THE PARABLE OF THE TABERNACLE

J. L. FERGUSON

Published by Hayes Press

First published 1981

Second and Revised Edition 2010

This Edition Copyright © 2018 HAYES PRESS. All rights reserved.

No part of this book may be used or reproduced by any means, graphic, electronic or mechanical, including photocopying, recording or by any information storage retrieval system without the written permission of the publisher except in the case of brief quotations embodied in critical articles and reviews.

All scripture quotations, unless otherwise indicated, are taken from the New King James Version. Copyright © 1979 onwards by Thomas Nelson, Inc. Used by permission. All rights reserved.

Published by HAYES PRESS

The Barn, Flaxlands,

Royal Wootton Bassett,

Swindon, UK, SN4 8DY

www.hayespress.org

t. +44 (0)1793 850598

e. info@hayespress.org

www.facebook.com/hayespress.org

http://twitter.com/#!/hayespress

FOREWORD TO THE FIRST EDITION

The typical teaching of the Tabernacle that God instructed Moses to build has occupied a central place in the exposition of the truth of Churches of God. These churches in the Fellowship of God's Son, the Lord Jesus Christ, together form the House of God on earth today. The writer of the Epistle to the Hebrews, when developing the concept of a spiritual people collectively drawing near to God through their Great High Priest in divine service, taught important and fundamental lessons from the Tabernacle in the wilderness. The shadow has given way to the substance but the reality of the true can be more deeply appreciated by a study of the type.

The late Mr. George Prasher's book, The Tabernacle or The Lord's Dwelling Place, which comprised a series of articles previously published in Needed Truth, became a reference book of immense value. Memory of our dear brother will always be precious as we associate with him his sound and telling Tabernacle ministry. Eternity alone will declare the fruits of his labour of love on this subject. Unfortunately, this book is now out of print and it was felt to be desirable and essential to have available for the rising generations, until the Lord comes back for His own, a further study of this vital truth. Our esteemed brother Mr. J. L. Ferguson was, therefore, invited to set down in writing the fruits of his meditation and rich ministry on this subject over many years.

We warmly commend to your prayerful study and reading The Parable of the Tabernacle and are greatly indebted to the author for his absorbing and vibrant presentation. To those in Churches of God we are assured it will prove to be for the building up of yourselves on your most holy faith (Jude 20). All Bible students, and others seeking truth and desirous of being guided and led by the Holy Spirit, will see it as part of the divine revelation in the New Testament - a portion of the whole counsel of God.

A careful study of this book will enable the reader to discern the two main objectives of the author. A clear vision of the House of God today as a called-out and gathered-together people in Churches of God, serving Him in Holy and Royal Priesthood service. Also, a more wonderful appreciation of the beauties, glories, character and functions of the lovely person of our Lord Jesus Christ who is Son over God's house (Heb.3:6).

'For whatever things were written before were written for our learning, that we through the patience and comfort of the Scriptures might have hope' (Rom.15:4).

'Now all these things happened to them as examples, and they were written for our admonition, upon whom the ends of the ages have come' (1 Cor.10:11).

L.H. Taylor 1981

FOREWORD TO THE SECOND EDITION

Some thirty years have passed since the publication of Mr. J.L. Ferguson's booklet The Parable of the Tabernacle and it was thought appropriate that it be reprinted. Mr. Ferguson died in 1989 and so the task of preparing this second edition has passed to others. Care has been taken, however, to ensure that the book remains substantially the same as the original in concept, content, and interpretation. The principal change is that quotations are now from the New King James Version of the Bible and not from the Revised Version, which is now out of print.

This required some minor changes to ensure the main text is consistent with the NKJV. Minor additions, aimed at helping the reader, include identifying authors, source hymn-book and hymn number of those hymns which are partially quoted in the first edition. The publication sources of the relevant hymn-books are also acknowledged. The original illustrations have been reordered so that each is now placed adjacent to the text which they illustrate and re-numbered appropriately. Indexes to the diagram and tables have also been added.

Finally, at the end of the book, a reference list is given showing from where the various quotes and citations have been taken; these were not located consistently in the first edition. It should be noted that some references are to texts which themselves have gone through several editions and it cannot be said for certain which edition was originally used. Those given now will point the interested reader in the right direction.

The thrust and conclusions of Mr. Ferguson's original have been maintained and this little book is commended to new readers for their careful consideration, not just of an ancient temporary structure that has long since disappeared, but also of the significance of what it teaches of the Lord Jesus Christ and the worship of God. The writer of the letter to the Hebrews describes the Tabernacle as being '... symbolic for the present time' (Heb. 9:9); Mr. Ferguson's exposition of its teaching has lost none of its relevance over the intervening years.

M.S. Elliott for General Literature Editors (December 2009)

ACKNOWLEDGEMENTS

Special acknowledgement is made of Mr. N.J.M. Miller (Glasgow) for the use of his painting of the Tabernacle for artwork and to Mr. W. Smyth (Glasgow) for the illustration of the tribes round the Tabernacle.

Special thanks to Mr. H. Leigh, M.A. (Oxon) for his time and kind assistance in photography of the furniture of the Tabernacle model.

CHAPTER 1: THE HEAVENLY THINGS THEMSELVES

'Open my eyes, that I may see wondrous things from Your law'. So wrote the Psalmist. As we approach our present study we do so in the spirit of his prayer. Our desire is to discover from the Scriptures lessons for ourselves from the Tabernacle that the Lord instructed the people of Israel to make under the guidance of His faithful servant Moses.

Details of the instructions are found in Exodus chapters 25-31 and of the erection in chapters 35-40, the whole structure being completed according to the divine pattern on the first day of the first month of the second year of the emancipated people of God. The structure of the building, the service of the sanctuary and the priesthood, all belong to an order of things which is rich in typical teaching with regard to the Son of God and His work, and with regard also to the will of God for an earthly people. It is therefore not surprising that the Holy Spirit directs our minds to regard it as one of the great parables of Scripture, full of teaching for our day.

We note too first of all that the Tabernacle is described in the New Testament as:

> "... the copy and shadow of the heavenly things" (Heb.8:5),
>
> "... copies of the things in the heavens" (Heb.9:23),
>
> "... copies of the true" (Heb.9:24).

Clearly then there is a great original in heaven, on which the earthly copy was based. We note that in Revelation 7:15; 11:19; 14:15; 15:5 and 16:17 John saw in his vision on Patmos a Temple in heaven. In this Temple, or related to it, he saw also:

- seven lamps of fire (4:5),
- a sea of glass (4:6),
- around the throne, the living creatures (5:11),
- the throne of God (7:15),
- the golden altar (8:3),
- the (bronze) altar (8:5),
- the ark of His covenant (11:19),

which things all have counterparts in the Tabernacle arrangement.

It would appear therefore that this Temple was the heavenly substance of which the Tabernacle in the wilderness was the shadow. That is not to say that the heavenly Temple is composed of the same kind of material from which the earthly Tabernacle was made. Heavenly things are beyond our tiny apprehension. This earth knows of no gold like that of the New Jerusalem, which in its purity is "... like transparent glass" (Rev.21:21).

This heavenly Temple is itself described in the epistle to the Hebrews as:

> "... the sanctuary and ... the true tabernacle which the Lord erected, and not man" (Heb.8:2),

> "the good things to come ... the greater and more perfect tabernacle not made with hands, that is, not of this creation" (Heb.9:11),

> "... the Most Holy Place" (Heb.9:12) better translated "the holies",

> "... the heavenly things themselves" (Heb.9:23).

In the services of the Tabernacle God's people walked among the shadows of the true.

CHAPTER 2: LET THEM MAKE ME A SANCTUARY

"Thus says the LORD: "Heaven is My throne, and earth is My footstool. Where is the house that you will build Me? And where is the place of My rest?"' (Is.66:1).

For some 2,500 years from the days of Eden God waited. In a world of rampant sin He walked with the men and women of faith who raised their family altar and sought forgiveness in the blood of their sacrifice. In Abraham at last He found a rock from which His long-term purposes could be hewn. Abraham had originally two sons. One of these God chose. Isaac had two sons. Again one of these God chose. Jacob had twelve sons. All of these God chose and from them in due course came the nation of Israel.

Included among the great purposes of God with regard to His people Israel was His desire that they would make Him a sanctuary so that He might dwell among them. Accordingly when they had been redeemed by the blood of the lambs in Egypt and had crossed the Red Sea, they came to Sinai where they entered into a covenant as a holy nation with Jehovah. The divine command then came to them: "... let them make Me a sanctuary, that I may dwell among them" (Ex.25:8).

The Lord gave to Moses the detailed pattern to which the Tabernacle and its furniture had to be made. Neither variation of nor departure from this was allowed (Ex.25:40). There was to be no scope for human ingenuity in its manufacture or construction, and Moses, the faithful servant in this wonderful work, adhered absolutely to the divine instructions. He co-ordinated the work of erection and, on completion, the glory of the Lord filled the Tabernacle, thus signifying His approval and at the same time realising His great desire to take up His abode among His people (see Ex.40:18-38).

What in effect then existed upon the earth, when the Tabernacle was erected, was something that had a correspondence with the Temple in heaven. That it was not the very image of the heavenly Temple is obvious, for the glory of the celestial is one and the glory of the terrestrial is another. But it exactly corresponded to the pattern (Acts 7:44; Heb.8:5) shown to Moses on the mount; the word being a translation of the Greek word 'tupos'. This word is also found in John 20:25 as the 'print' of the nails. There were real nails answering to the wound prints.

What Moses erected on the desert sands was in perfect keeping with the instructions he received: 'According to all that I show you, that is, the pattern of the tabernacle and the pattern of all its furnishings, just so you shall make it' (Ex.25:9). Hence the sevenfold comment in the erection record of Exodus 40: '... as the LORD had commanded Moses'.

CHAPTER 3: SYMBOLIC FOR THE PRESENT TIME

In both Testaments of the Bible there are many parables. The Lord Jesus frequently illustrated His teaching by referring to a well-known feature in nature or a happening in everyday life. By laying something His hearers understood alongside something they had not yet perceived, they could be helped to grasp the teaching. The Tabernacle must surely be the most remarkable and detailed of all the Bible parables and one wonders whether it was only time and space which precluded the writer to the Hebrews from giving a detailed exposition and application of its several parts (Heb.9:5). The Lord Jesus, Himself the Master of all parable teaching, taught us to look for instruction in detail (Matt.13:18-23). This then will guide us in our study; at the same time avoiding the mistake of thinking that everything must have a meaning.

Hebrews 9:9 says of the first Tabernacle, that is the Holy Place, that it is, '... symbolic for the present time'. The parable becomes more expansive as we consider that the Holy Place was inseparably associated with the altar and the laver in the courtyard, and its hanging veil connected it immediately with the Most Holy Place within. So in all the articles and forms of service in the first of all God's earthly dwelling places we can see illustrated many precious aspects of the service of God in His dwelling place today.

Some have viewed this matter of shadow and substance as what we find described in Colossians 2:16,17; and so teach that the Tabernacle was the shadow and that Christ is the substance. To a great extent this is true and we shall find that many things, particularly the materials from which it was made, portray beautifully the excellencies of our Lord Jesus Christ. There is however much more to Tabernacle teaching. From it God would teach us vital present-day principles with regard to His dwelling place among a redeemed and gathered together people.

This search for what answers in 'the present time' to the typical teaching of the Tabernacle will involve frequent reference to the house, sanctuary and service of God in both the Old and the New Testaments. It may therefore be helpful at this point to consider in brief detail how the old order of things gave place in due course to the new.

CHAPTER 4: IN THE DAYS OF THE SHADOWS

One of the jewels in the crown of Israel was undoubtedly '... the service of God' (Rom. 9:4). It stood related to the law of Sinai, the sanctuary of God and the priesthood of Aaron. It continued for a period of some 1,500 years until the resurrection of the Lord Jesus Christ. For some 500 years it was associated with the Tabernacle and for the remainder of the period with the Temples of Solomon, the remnant, and Herod the king.

It all began with God redeeming the descendants of Jacob in the land of Egypt by the blood of the Passover lambs. Then He delivered them out from Egypt by what He later described as their baptism to Moses in the cloud and in the waters of the Red Sea (1 Cor.10:2). He led them straight to Mount Sinai and there made with them a covenant of obedience, described in Exodus 19-24. He accepted them as His separated people, describing them as '... a special treasure to Me above all people' (Ex.19:5), a kingdom of priests and a holy nation, but strictly conditional on their obedience to His voice and the keeping of His covenant. They pledged their obedience in the well-known words, 'All that the LORD has said we will do, and be obedient' (Ex.24:7).

The response from God was immediate: '... let them make Me a sanctuary, that I may dwell among them' (Ex.25:8). Thus, the Old Testament people of God were brought into being. The God who was with them in their redemption in Egypt, was for them in their baptism at the Red Sea, was now to be in the midst of them as a separated, covenanted people, at Sinai.

Before this, as children of Abraham through Isaac and Jacob, they already had assured to them unconditionally the benefits of the covenant-promise given by God to Abraham, guaranteeing the Seed and the land to perpetuity (Gen.15; Gal.3:16). Now at Sinai they entered into a new covenant relationship, involving responsibility for the service of God in His earthly sanctuary. But this time the covenant was conditional on their obedience. They could never lose the benefits of the covenant of Abraham, but they could forfeit the blessings of the covenant of Sinai.

The nation of Israel had then entered on the service of God. They were a kingdom of priests and were all invited to participate in varying degrees in the service. The people generally could come as far as the altar that stood in the courtyard surrounding the Tabernacle. There they brought their offerings of appreciation or their sacrifices for sin. They were represented in the service of the sanctuary by Aaron and his male descendants, assisted by the remainder of the men of age of the tribe of Levi. The priests and Levites had the right of entry to the first of the two sections of the Tabernacle, called the Holy Place, accomplishing various services. But the high priest alone could enter the second section, the Most Holy Place, and that only on the annual Day of Atonement.

Century after century the worshippers brought, and the priests offered, the same sacrifices continually. Century after century the dividing veil hung there; the nation coming only as far as the altar, the priests to the Holy Place only, and the high priest once in the year within the veil to the place of the mercy seat. It was evident that the law of Sinai '... made nothing perfect' (Heb.7:19). It was '... imposed until the time of reformation' (Heb.9:10).

CHAPTER 5: THE SHINING OF THE TRUE LIGHT

Some 1,500 years passed and at last the fullness of the time came and God sent forth His Son. His life span was somewhat less than thirty-four years and culminated in an atoning death that was wonderful in achievement. Among many other things, it cleansed the sanctuary of God in heaven (Heb.9:23) in readiness for a new holy nation, which took the place of Israel, to draw near; and it perfected for ever those who are sanctified through faith in Him (Heb.10:14).

In His resurrection, Jesus the Son of God was appointed by God '... a priest forever according to the order of Melchizedek' (Heb.7:17). This change in the priesthood brought of necessity a change also in the law (Heb.7:12) and in the service of God. The priesthood of Aaron gave place to that of the Lord Jesus Christ. The law of Moses gave place to the faith once for all delivered to the saints. The service in material things, related to a physical dwelling place of God, gave place to that of the spiritual house of living stones, enjoying access to the heavenly sanctuary. The old order had gone. The house of God had become at last, in reality, the gate of heaven.

In His priestly service the Lord Jesus became an Advocate for all God's children (1 Jn.2:1) and a great High Priest for God's people (Heb.4:14). How individual children of God became the collective people of God is an instructive study in the New Testament and the matter will arise from time to time in this study. It was the practical out-working of the Lord's prayer in John 17:21 together with His commission to the apostles in Matthew 28:19,20.

At conversion every believer was given eternal life (Jn.3:36), unconditional security (Jn.10:28), and a place in the Church, which is His Body (1 Cor.12:13). Baptism by immersion in water invariably followed immediately. Then in order to give effect to the Lord's commission, the disciples were added initially to the first Church of God, in Jerusalem, and subsequently to churches of God elsewhere, so that they could be taught their Lord's will and give effect to it in their lives.

The progressive steps in the will of God for the disciples of the Lord Jesus Christ, then and now, are set out in remarkable clarity, and in all the precision of the divine order, in Acts 2:41,42: 'Then those who gladly received his word were baptized; and that day about three thousand souls were added to them. And they continued steadfastly in the apostles' doctrine and (Gk - the) fellowship, (Gk - and) in the breaking of bread, and in (Gk - the) prayers.'

The Church of God in Jerusalem was one church, irrespective of the number of its meeting places. A comparison can usefully be made of Acts 8:1 and 1 Corinthians 15:9. It was composed solely of baptized believers who were added together with a view to permanent testimony. When Saul of Tarsus, '... tried to join the disciples' (Acts 9:26) in the Church of God in Jerusalem, the word means to glue together.

It was under the care of one group of elders, as seen in Acts 15:2. As the work of the Lord spread, it did so on the basis of a uniform teaching and practice (1 Cor.4:17; 11:16). Indeed Romans 6:17 describes the disciples as, at conversion, having '... obeyed from the heart that form of doctrine to which you were delivered.' Thus, all the churches were built to the same pattern, mould or form.

Not only so, but the churches were themselves in unity, a fellowship of assemblies, as Israel had been a fellowship of tribes. So we read of:

- The churches of Judea (Gal.1:22);
- The churches throughout all Judea, Galilee and Samaria (Acts 9:31);
- The churches of Galatia (Gal.1:2);

THE PARABLE OF THE TABERNACLE

- The churches of Asia (1 Cor.16:19);
- The churches of Macedonia (2 Cor.8:1);
- The churches of Achaia (2 Cor.9:2);
- The pilgrims of the Dispersion in Pontus, Galatia, Cappadocia, Asia, and Bithynia (1 Pet.1:1);
- The fellowship of His Son, Jesus Christ our Lord (1 Cor.1:9).

Thus, the kingdom of God was taken away from Israel and given to a nation which would bear the fruits of it (Matt.21:43); given to the 'little flock' seen in embryo in Luke 12:32. In the churches of God, as distinct from the Church, which is His Body:

> '... living stones, are being built up a spiritual house, a holy priesthood, to offer up spiritual sacrifices acceptable to God through Jesus Christ ... a chosen generation, a royal priesthood, a holy nation, His own special people, that you may proclaim the praises of Him who called you out of darkness into His marvellous light; who once were not a people but are now the people of God' (1 Pet.2:5,9,10).

The New Testament churches of God were a unity, and, conditional on their obedience (Heb. 3:6), God's spiritual house. They had, as a great High Priest, Jesus the Son of God. They were invited to come boldly in collective prayer to the throne of grace (Heb.4:14-16). They were invited also to enter with boldness into the Holies in collective worship (Heb.10:19-22). They were God's spiritual house on earth, with their place of Godward service the sanctuary in the heavens.

So when, '... a great many of the priests were obedient to the faith' (Acts 6:7), they left behind them a ministry of material things in a material house and earthly sanctuary to become living stones in a spiritual house, sharing in a ministry of spiritual services which, stood related to the heavenly sanctuary. This was the 'holy priesthood' aspect of their service. In addition, as 'a royal priesthood' they had committed to them the word of reconciliation. With this, as the Lord's ambassadors, they entreated the people by the preaching of the excellencies of the Lord Jesus.

CHAPTER 6: PRINCIPLES OF INTERPRETATION

How, then, is the great Tabernacle parable to be interpreted? We read, for example, of '... the veil, that is, His flesh' (Heb.10:20). But beyond that, no specific guidance is given in Scripture as to principles of interpretation. Extremely fanciful lines have been followed by some teachers, whereas others have shared the view of P. Fairbairn that, '... in regard to the articles used, it does not appear that any higher reason can be assigned for their selection, than that they were the best and fittest of their several kinds'[1]

We must certainly avoid dogmatism. There has been, however, fairly general support for the view that since the Spirit describes the Tabernacle as a parable, and indeed interprets the veil, we are entitled to anticipate a wide variety of typical teaching for the present day. This is best put forward suggestively and reasonably substantiated. Two principles must certainly be adhered to. One is that once an interpretation has been given to part of the parable, it must be understood only in that sense throughout. The other is that teaching developed from the type must be in harmony with New Testament principles. The following then is our understanding of the typical teaching of the materials used in the making of the Tabernacle.

- **Fine linen thread (RV: fine twined linen)** - divine righteousness, which may also be imputed to or wrought out by the believer (note Ps.132:9; Rev.19:8). The Hebrew root of the word linen is from 'to bleach' or 'to whiten'.
- **Blue** - of heavenly character. In Ezekiel 10:1 the sapphire stone was the emblem of God's throne and sapphires, like the unclouded skies, are pure, deep blue.
- **Purple** - of royal dignity. The blending colour from blue to

scarlet was the colour of kings (see Judg.8:26).
- **Scarlet** - of lowly, sacrificial order. The Hebrew word is translated crimson, scarlet, worm; giving the thought of sacrifice (Lev.14:4; Num.19:6; Is.1:18) and of despising (Ps.22:6). Note - the order of the three colours never changes. The sequence of the group of four does - hence the next two points:
- **Blue, and purple, and scarlet, and fine linen thread** - the Lord Jesus Christ in the excellencies of His Manhood.
- **Fine linen thread, and blue, and purple, and scarlet** - disciples in the house of God reflecting the excellencies of the Lord Jesus Christ.
- **Gold** - the glory of Deity - the metal being descriptive of supreme excellency in many places in Scripture. For example, the coming City of God has '... the glory of God' and is '... pure gold' (Rev.21:11,18). It is the first metal to be mentioned in Scripture (Gen.2:11,12).
- **Silver** - redemption in its various aspects (see the Atonement money in Ex.30:11-16 and 1 Pet.1:18).
- **Bronze (see Note)** - durability and strength (as in Judg.16:21; 1 Sam.17:5,6; Job 40:18) or judgement (as in Rev.1:15 and note Num.16:36-40). Relevant to this is copper's ability to endure fierce heat, its melting point approaching 1100°C.
- **Acacia wood** - the humanity of the Lord, who in death '... saw no corruption' (Acts 13:37); and in another sense, disciples who have '... been born again, not of corruptible seed but incorruptible' (1 Pet.1:23). Jerome wrote of the acacia tree, 'It is a tree which grows in the desert, like a white thorn in colour and leaves, not in size. For they are of such size, that very large planks are cut out of them. The wood is very strong, and of incredible lightness and beauty' (Pusey on Joel, p.242)[2]. Josephus says it could not, 'suffer corruption'.[3] The

Septuagint simply calls it 'incorruptible wood'. The KJV refers to shittim wood, shittim deriving from a word meaning 'to scourge'.

- **Goats' hair** - the word hair is inserted for clarity but is not in the original Hebrew. It stimulates the thought of the sin-bearing goats on the Day of Atonement (see Lev.16).
- **Ram skins dyed red** - consecration to the point of death in the service of God (See Ex.29:31).
- **Badger skins** - the Person of the Lord Jesus, similarly the outward appearance of the house of God, unattractive to many, and unappreciated by them.
- **Embroidered cherubim** - symbols of the sentinels of the holiness of God, as originally in Ezekiel 28:14.
- **Horns** - strength and authority, as in 2 Samuel 22:3; Amos 6:13 RV.
- **Oil** - the Holy Spirit, as seen, for example, in the composite vision of Zechariah 4 and in the anointing of the Lord Jesus with the Spirit of the Lord in Luke 4:18.

In the chapters which follow there will be no need to restate in detail the foregoing reasons for the application of the various types.

It must be appreciated that varying views are held on the details of the typology of the Tabernacle generally. These must be respected where soundly, scripturally based. In their ministry, others can also develop points of detail with which it is not practicable to deal with in this brief study.

Note:

The Hebrew word nechosheth is variously translated in different versions of the Bible. In both the AV and RV it is translated 'brass'; in the NIV and NKJV it is rendered 'bronze' (Strong's OT:5178). Both are alloys of copper. Brass is an alloy of copper and zinc, whereas in bronze, copper is alloyed with tin. It is now impossible to know whether the base metal components of the Tabernacle were fashioned from pure copper or one of its alloys. Bronze is used in this edition, following the usage of the NKJV from which quotations are taken. The Greek word chalkos is translated 'brass' in KJV, RV, NIV, and NKJV (Strong's NT:5475).[4] Vine comments that, although primarily referring to copper it, '... became used for metals in general, later was applied to bronze'.

CHAPTER 7: THE OVERALL ARRANGEMENT

Balaam, looking down on the encampment of Israel arranged according to their tribes, was impressed by its order and symmetry and said, 'How lovely are your tents, O Jacob! Your dwellings, O Israel! Like valleys that stretch out, like gardens by the riverside, like aloes planted by the LORD, like cedars beside the waters' (Num.24:5,6).

Whether Israel was encamped in the wilderness or on the march through it, they were grouped in a precision laid down by God. Over the Tabernacle was the token of the divine presence, the pillar of cloud by day, becoming fire by night. '... and in the place where the cloud settled, there the children of Israel would pitch their tents. At the command of the LORD the children of Israel would journey, and at the command of the LORD they would camp; as long as the cloud stayed above the tabernacle they remained encamped' (Num.9:17,18). They had no difficulty about guidance. The cloud was to be their guide.

The layout of the encampment was by order of the One who, centuries later came in Manhood, and said, 'Make them sit down in groups of fifty' (Lk.9:14). The order is described in Numbers 2,3 and is best shown in the following diagram:

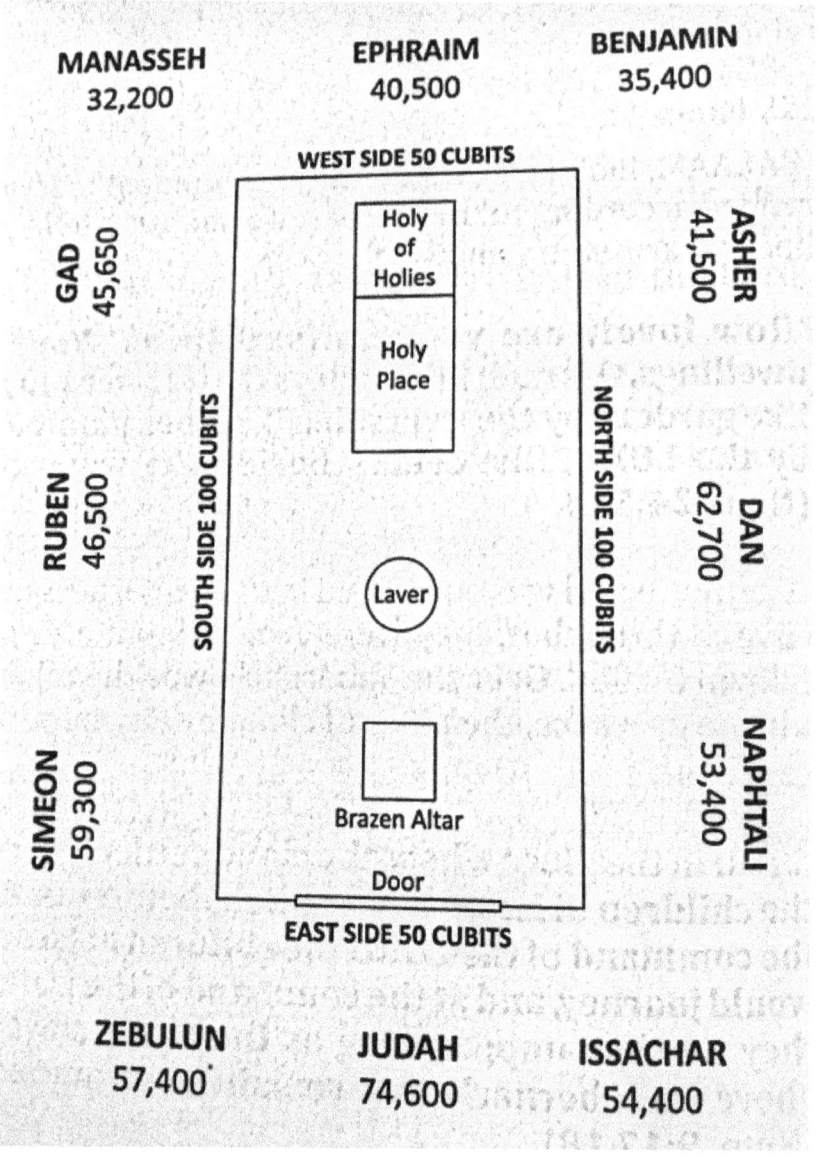

The nation camped round the sanctuary: 'I AM' was in the midst of His people, '... glorious in holiness, fearful in praises, doing wonders' (Ex.

15:11) as Moses foresaw on the bank of the Red Sea. The dwelling place was known as:

- Ex.25:8 - A sanctuary (i.e., a holy or consecrated place),
- Ex.25:9 - The tabernacle (i.e., a dwelling place),
- Ex.34:26 - The house of the LORD,
- Ex.38:21 - The tabernacle of the Testimony (i.e., witness),
- Ex.39:38 - The tabernacle ('RV: the Tent')
- Ex.40:12 - The tabernacle of meeting (not to be confused with the tent of this name in Exodus 33:7 and 38:8).

It was thus God's house and sanctuary, the place where He met with His people; being also a witness to the existing covenant with Israel as well as a testimony to things to come. It was a rectangle with its longer sides orientated east-west, and with its door at the east, towards the sun-rising, for the arrangement was pointing forward to the dawn of the day of the better things. It was thirty cubits long, ten cubits wide, and ten cubits high (see Table of Measurements.) The first section, the Holy Place, measured twenty cubits long, ten cubits wide and ten cubits high; the Most Holy Place, a cube of ten cubits. It was set in a court, surrounded by hangings which measured one hundred cubits long, fifty cubits wide and five cubits high. All cubic measurements were in multiples of five.

In front of the entrance, keeping the charge of the sanctuary, were the tents of Moses and of Aaron and his sons. Behind the Tabernacle, westward, camped the families of the Gershonites; southward the Kohathites; northwards the Merarites. This position of great excellence was given to these three families, the Levites as they were called, as a reward for consecration on the day of the golden calf, when Moses called from the gate of the camp, 'Whoever is on the LORD'S side - come to me!' (Ex.32:26).

They were promised a blessing that day, and it was granted to them in Numbers 3:6, when God said, 'Bring the tribe of Levi near'. Levi means 'joined'. And in place of the firstborn sons, who failed in the matter of the call of Moses, the Levites were joined to the sons of Aaron with a solemn charge in the service of God. Then ranging round the four sides was the vast, orderly arrangement of the tents of the twelve tribes, Joseph's two sons both being given tribal recognition. When in due course the ark crossed Jordan (Josh.3:4) there was a space of 2000 cubits between it and the people; so the tribes may have camped well back from the Tabernacle.

The correspondence of the whole layout with the heavenly scene presented in Hebrews 12:18-29 is so striking that it may well be that the pattern shown to Moses on the mount included an arrangement of the angelic hosts which Moses faithfully followed in the ordering of the nation round the sanctuary. Thus, the '... innumerable company of angels ... the general assembly and church of the firstborn (firstborn ones, Greek is plural) who are registered in heaven' (Heb.12:22,23), were seen in the twelve tribes of the national host, and the inner grouping of Levites, carefully numbered or enrolled in place of the firstborn sons in Numbers 3:40-51.

According to Numbers 33, the nation journeyed and pitched in the wilderness over 40 times; for some 38 years wandering in the region of Kadesh-Barnea. The order of the march was just as precise as that of the encampment and is outlined in Numbers 2,3,4,10 as:

- The Camp of Judah, being in order the three tribes: Judah, Issachar, Zebulun,
- The Gershonites bearing the Tabernacle curtains, screens and court hangings etc.,
- The Merarites bearing the boards, bars, pillars etc.,
- The Camp of Reuben, being in order the three tribes: Reuben,

Simeon, Gad,
- The Kohathites in the midst bearing the vessels of the sanctuary,
- The Camp of Ephraim, being in order the three tribes: Ephraim, Manasseh, Benjamin,
- The Camp of Dan, being in order the three tribes: Dan, Asher, Naphtali.

In this remarkable order Judah always went first (see also Judg.1:1,2), for Judah means 'praise' and this has the pre-eminent place in the service of God. The Merarites and the Gershonites went ahead of the Kohathites so that by the time the latter arrived the former had the Tabernacle erected ready to receive the articles of service. The Gershonites had two wagons and four oxen to assist them in transport. The Merarites had four wagons and eight oxen (Num.7). But to the Kohathites belonged the service of the sanctuary and they carried its sacred vessels on their shoulders.

The various articles were covered by cloths of blue and scarlet and purple and, except for the ark, had badger skin coverings on top. The ark's covering cloth of blue was left topmost. Central to the great march as it filed through the wilderness was the ark of the covenant in its outstandingly distinguishable covering of blue (Num.4). Thus, even in the march, God saw the shadows of His Son in the midst of His people and was content to walk with them (2 Sam.7:6).

CHAPTER 8: SEQUENCE OF STUDY

There are two portions that deal specifically with the instructions to Moses for the making of the Tabernacle and subsequently with its construction. Each occupies six and five chapters respectively in Exodus. It indicates the importance God attaches to His house when we consider that the first ten chapters of Genesis cover by contrast a very long period of human history.

For easy reference, the following are the two orders:

Order of instruction

1. Ex. 25:10-22 - The ark of the Testimony
2. Ex. 25:23-30 - The table of showbread
3. Ex. 25:31-40 - The lampstand
4. Ex. 26:1-6 - Tabernacle curtains
5. Ex. 26:7-13 - Goats' hair curtains
6. Ex. 26:14 - Overall coverings
7. Ex. 26:15-30 - Boards and bars
8. Ex. 26:31-35 - The veil
9. Ex. 26:36-37 - Screen for tent door
10. Ex. 27:1-8 - The altar of burnt offering
11. Ex. 27:9-19 - Hangings of court and gate
12. Ex. 27:20-21 - Oil for the lamps
13. Ex.28 - Garments of priests
14. Ex.29 - Consecration of priests
15. Ex. 30:1-10 - The altar of incense
16. Ex. 30:17-21 - The laver
17. Ex. 30:22-33 - The holy anointing oil
18. Ex. 30:34-38 - The incense

Order of construction

THE PARABLE OF THE TABERNACLE

1. Ex.36:8-13 - Tabernacle curtains

2. Ex.36:14-18 - Goats' hair curtains

3. Ex.36:19 - Overall coverings

4. Ex.36:20-34 - Boards and bars

5. Ex.36:35-36 - The veil

6. Ex.36:37-38 - Screen for door of tent

7. Ex.37:1-9 - The ark of the Testimony

8. Ex.37:10-16 - The table of showbread

9. Ex.37:17-24 - The lampstand

10. Ex.37:25-28 - The altar of incense

11. Ex.37:29 - The holy anointing oil

12. Ex.37:29 - The incense

13. Ex.38:1-7 - The altar of burnt offering

14. Ex.38:8 - The laver

15. Ex.38:9-20 - Hangings of court and gate

16. Ex.39:1-31 - Garments of priests

17. Ex.40 - Consecration of priests and erection of Tabernacle

While Moses was forty days at Mount Sinai receiving the instructions defining the inner sanctuary which would enshrine the holiness of God, and the various garments which would adorn the priests, Aaron the prospective high priest, was leading the people in an orgy of fleshly sin and the people were dancing beside the golden calf which Aaron had made from their golden ear-rings. They said, 'This is your god, O Israel, that brought you out of the land of Egypt!' (Ex.32:4). Aaron said, 'Tomorrow is a feast to the LORD' (Ex.32:5).

What utter confusion! Who else but the God whom we have come through grace to know would have allowed His plans to develop with a people perverse from the beginning. But He would allow no acts of human wilfulness to deflect Him from His purpose to dwell with His people. He would abide with them until in the ultimate, '... there was no remedy' (2 Chr.36:16).

He recalled Moses, the princely interceder, to the mount and, after another forty days and nights, Moses returned and invited the repentant people to bring their offerings for the Lord's service. Eventually he had to restrain them. Then under the guidance of Bezalel and Aholiab, men filled with the Spirit of the Lord and wisdom for the work, the building began.

We note from the two columns that the various items as they were constructed, moving outward from the central ark in the presence of God, are not listed in the same order when their construction is detailed. For that reason we do not feel bound to any particular order in dealing with them. We therefore propose to move from the outside hangings through to within the veil, to the ark of the Testimony.

CHAPTER 9: TABLE OF MEASUREMENTS

The cubit sizes quoted in Scripture are used throughout this study. For ease of reference there is noted below these sizes where given, and assuming the cubit to equal 18 inches, the relative sizes in linear yards and metres are placed alongside. The sequence is length, breadth and height as appropriate.

- The hangings of the court: 100x50x5 cubits / 50x25x2.5 yards / 45.72x22.86x2.29 metres
- The gate of the court: 20x5 cubits/ 10x2.5 yards / 9.14x2.29 metres
- The bronze altar: 5x5x3 cubits / 2.5x2.5x1.5 yards / 2.29x2.29x1.37 metres
- Each Tabernacle curtain: 28x4 cubits / 14x2 yards / 12.80x1.83 metres
- Total curtain area: 28x40 cubits / 14x20 yards / 12.80x18.28 metres
- Each goats' hair curtain: 30x4 cubits / 15x2 yards / 13.72x1.83 metres
- Total goats' hair area: 30x44 cubits / 15x22 yards / 13.72x20.12 metres
- Each board: 1.5x10 cubits / 0.75x5 yards / 0.69x4.57 metres

Total board area

- North and South sides: 30x10 cubits / 15x5 yards / 13.72x4.57 metres
- West side plus supporting boards: 10x10 cubits/ 5x5 yards / 4.57x4.57 metres
- The screen for the door of the tent (approx.): 10x10 cubits /

5x5 yards / 4.57x4.57 metres
- The veil (approx.): 10x10 cubits/ 5x5 yards / 4.57x4.57 metres
- The table of showbread: 2x1x1.5 cubits / 1x0.5x0.75 yards / 0.91x0.46x0.69 metres
- The altar of incense: 1x1x2 cubits / 0.5x0.5x1 yards / 0.46x0.46x0.91 metres
- The ark of the Testimony: 2.5x1.5x1.5 cubits / 1.25x0.75x0.75 yards / 1.14x0.69x0.69 metres
- The mercy seat: 2.5x1.5 cubits/ 1.25x0.75 yards / 1.14x0.69 metres
- The lampstand: No measurements given.
- The laver: No measurements given.

CHAPTER 10: THE HANGINGS OF THE COURT

Exodus 27:9-19; 38:9-20

In the dawn of human history God communed with Adam and Eve in the Garden of Eden. The word translated 'garden' means a place fenced in or hedged about for protection. The serpent came in from the field. The sinful pair were in due course driven out from the garden. The place of divine communion had thus a clearly defined boundary with an entrance at the east side. The briefly depicted scene closes with the cherubim and the flaming sword 'placed' (the same word as to 'dwell' in Ex.25:8) at the gate, guarding the way to the tree of life, as against another day when One would come, sheathe the sword in Himself, and open up the way to God and to eternal life, for all who would believe in Him.

The Tabernacle also was a place fenced in. It was placed in a court, enclosed by what were termed hangings, measuring one hundred cubits long, fifty cubits broad and five cubits high. The thought in the word court is to 'surround with a stockade' or 'enclose by a fence'. The hangings in effect fenced in the dwelling place of God. The entrance, termed the gate of the court, was on the east side, facing the sunrise. This was a screen measuring twenty cubits broad and, of course, five cubits high in common with the hangings. It was the first of three entrances, leading to areas of increasing holiness.

All the hangings were made of fine linen thread but the gate was made of blue, and purple, and scarlet and fine linen thread, the work of the embroiderer. The hangings were supported by pillars, twenty on both the north and south sides, ten on the west and east sides. On the east side, four supported the gate, with three on either side for the hangings.

What the pillars were made of is not stated. They were probably made of acacia wood unless Exodus 27:10,18,19 indicates bronze.

All the sixty pillars rested on sockets of bronze. They were connected at the top by what were termed bands (from a word meaning 'to join'), made of silver, and capped by capitals overlaid with silver. Silver hooks kept the hangings in position and pins of copper with cords kept the pillars in place.

Job had long before said: 'Oh, that I knew where I might find Him, that I might come to His seat!' (Job 23:3). Men of Job's spiritual insight had met God at their altar by their homes. The principle dated back to the expulsion from Eden when Abel 'brought' his offering, indicating a special place. But now, within these hangings, was the divinely appointed place of approach in worship and service. The appointed bounds at Sinai had prevented the people from drawing near. There were still appointed bounds to the presence of God in the Tabernacle. But the wide gate invited all Israel to approach. The nation was called to the altar in the court; the priests and the Levites to the laver and the service within the sanctuary.

Everywhere the holiness and righteousness of God were in evidence - the pillar of cloud and fire, the whiteness of the surrounding hangings, the leaping flames on the altar within the gate. But within the court the worshipper could find a place of acceptance as he came with his offering; sometimes for thanksgiving, sometimes for sin; sometimes all for God, sometimes the offerer and his family sharing as they ate together in the safety of the court. Although this was as near to the sanctuary of God as David ever reached, yet with joy he could say: 'And I will dwell in the house of the LORD forever' (Ps.23:6).

But in it all lay a parable for our own day. A repentant man in search of God - by what means will he find Him? A believer in the Lord Jesus Christ in search of the sanctuary service of God - where and how will he find it? Born outside the gate; born in the enemy camp; therefore, confronting every man on every side is the righteousness of God to which he cannot by his own efforts attain. Fourteen points are listed in Romans 3:9-18 to show that by nature men are under sin and the judgement of God. The first of these is: 'There is none who does good, no, not one' (Rom.3:12). What could be more final?

The height of the curtains at five cubits clearly symbolized that the righteousness of God was high beyond human reach. It was also a righteousness founded on judgement, for the supporting pillars rested on sockets of bronze. These two attributes of God are inseparable. The psalmist wrote: 'You have executed justice and righteousness' (Ps.99:4); and again, 'Righteousness and justice are the foundation of Your throne' (Ps.89:14).

But joining the pillars together were the bands of silver, capped by the silver capitals. Here was a clear indication that it was the crowning glory of God to redeem. From all eternity He had planned a basis for the redemption of the human family from sin, in perfect harmony with the requirements of His principles of righteousness and judgement.

An interesting point here is that the word translated 'band' is also translated 'love' in Isaiah 38:17 RV; as the NKJV puts it: 'But You have lovingly delivered my soul. No wonder we sing:

> There's a way back to God from the dark paths of sin;
>
> There's a door that is open and you may go in:
>
> At Calvary's cross is where you begin,
>
> When you come as a sinner to Jesus.
>
> (E.H. Swinstead, CSSM)

That way back to God was symbolized in the one gate on the east side. It was the only break in the hangings of the court. It measured twenty cubits across; so it was wide, open and inviting, picturing so choicely the Lord Jesus Christ as the sinner's only way to God. He was the One who could answer to the holy requirements of the righteousness of God, even as the height of the gate corresponded to the height of the hangings. Here in the shadows was the Lord from heaven, the heavenly Man (the blue), of Israel's kingly line according to the flesh and regal in the nobility of all His ways (the purple), yet lowly withal, not here to be ministered to, but Himself dedicated in self-abnegation to the help of others (the scarlet), the righteous Servant of Jehovah, 'Who committed no sin...' (1 Pet.2:22) and to whom even Pilate the Roman judge gave a threefold testimony of innocence (the fine linen thread).

'Where is the way to the dwelling of light?' asked Job (Job 38:19). Here it was in the eastern gate. But who would deal with the cherubim and the sword of the first eastern gate, which guarded the way back to God? Only the Lord Jesus Christ could do this. And symbolized in the gate of the court we see Him in the perfection of His Manhood, ready to go to Calvary worthy to provide salvation for all who would accept Him as Saviour. So the message of the gate found an echo in His own words: 'I am ... the life. No one comes to the Father except through Me' (Jn.14:6). '... and the one who comes to Me I will by no means cast out' (Jn.6:37).

CHAPTER 11: THE BRONZE ALTAR OF BURNT OFFERING

Exodus 27:1-8; Exodus 38:1-7; Leviticus 6:8-13

Inside the gate of the court stood the altar of burnt offering. It dominated the court and could have contained all the other measured articles of furniture. God called It, 'My altar' (1 Sam.2:28). Sacrifice elsewhere to Him by His people was now no longer acceptable. This was the altar that would henceforth sanctify the gift. This was God's one altar.

It was made of planks of acacia wood overlaid with bronze. It was square in plan, measuring five cubits by five cubits and stood three cubits high. The altar itself was hollow but within it was probably the mound of earth previously legislated for in Exodus 20:24, on which the sacrifices would be laid, the hearth of Leviticus 6:9.

The altar had a grating of bronze network with a bronze ring in each corner. The rings were for the staves of acacia wood overlaid with bronze for use when the altar was in transit. There is doubt as to whether this grating was placed inside or outside the altar. It was positioned under a ledge placed halfway up the altar, exactly at the height of the mercy seat, with all that suggests. The narrative certainly reads as though the ledge was outside and under the ledge was the grating, as though the altar was in a basket with its staves for ease of transport. We do not press the point save to say that no matter how the grating is viewed, the removal of the ashes remains unexplained in the Word. But it may well be that to negotiate the sacrifices on an altar three cubits high the priest stood on this ledge. This would agree with Leviticus 9:22 without conflicting with Exodus 20:26.

On the top of each of the four corners of the altar was a horn, of one piece with the acacia structure and overlaid with bronze. Psalm 118:27 suggests that to these horns the sacrifices were bound with cords, but the word in the verse translated 'sacrifice' gives but slender support to the thought.

In addition there were attendant items for daily use in the altar service, such as shovels and basins for the ashes, basins for the blood, forks for handling the sacrifices and fire-pans to carry the altar fire when the camp was on the march. These accessories were all made of acacia wood overlaid with bronze.

The fire on the altar was unique and was never to go out. It was evidently fire, '... from before the LORD'. So long as God dwelt within His sanctuary among His people in abiding, burning holiness, so long was the altar fire to burn - which came down upon the altar at the commencement of the Tabernacle service (Lev. 9:24 and repeated at the dedication of Solomon's temple in 2 Chr.7:1) and was maintained by the continual wood offering of the people as referred to in Nehemiah 10:34 and elsewhere. So long as God dwelt within His sanctuary among His people in abiding, burning holiness, so long was the altar fire to burn.

But it was fire which was contained, not like the fires of judgement which came forth from the Lord and burned in the camp in the matter of Korah (Num. 16:35). In the darkness of the night, as the Israelites may have watched in the wilderness the spectacular lights in the Tabernacle court, men of faith would appreciate the relationship between the pillar of fire over the sanctuary, confirming the presence of the Holy One, and the leaping flames on the altar of burnt offering.

The first and greatest service at the bronze altar was the offering every morning and evening, by the command of the Lord, of Israel's national burnt offering. Each consisted of a lamb of the first year, with the tenth part of an ephah of flour mingled with the fourth part of a hin of pressed oil, and the fourth part of a hin of wine for a drink offering, with double quantities on the Sabbath (see Ex. 29:38-46).

It was Christ in the shadows; in life, in the fullness of the Spirit matched by the joy of the Lord, giving Himself in death. So the lambs burned daily as incense (in Lev.6:12 the first word 'burn' means, to burn as fuel; the second, to burn as incense) and by reason of the fragrance of the Lamb of God who would one day be crucified at the hour of the morning sacrifice and die at the hour of the evening oblation, God was willing to bear daily with wayward Israel.

The next great purpose of the bronze altar was that all the desires of Israel Godward might find tangible expression. Israel's best days were when the highways to Zion rejoiced as the pilgrims came from all parts of the land bringing their sacrifices.

The closer men walked with God, the more frequent would be their recourse to the altar. The next great purpose of the bronze altar was that all the desires of Israel Godward might find tangible expression. Israel's best days were when the highways to Zion rejoiced as the pilgrims came from all parts of the land bringing their sacrifices. Individuals were invited to come with their burnt offerings, their meal offerings, their peace offerings - all expressions of gratitude for grace received.

They were expected also to come with their sin and trespass offerings in acknowledgement of their transgression. The altar of burnt offering was therefore a measure of the spiritual condition of the people. The closer men walked with God, the more frequent would be their recourse to the altar. In all their givings, from the choice young bull, pride of the herd, for a burnt offering, to the tenth part of an ephah of fine flour for a sin offering, God enjoyed the fragrance of the one great Offering for whom He waited.

Again we consider the altar, this time in its typical setting. When the writer to the Hebrews said, 'We have an altar (Heb. 13:10), who else but the Lord Jesus could he have had in view? The remarkable thing is that we see in Him both the altar as well as the sacrifices which were offered on it. The altar does not foreshadow the Cross, but the Lord Jesus on the Cross enduring the judgement of God as He made the great atonement for sin and sinners.

It was hollow, for the Christ who was coming would empty Himself to dwell among us, leaving behind Him the glory which He had alongside the Father before worlds were made, coming in the glory of His moral and spiritual excellencies alone. And just as the breadth and length of the altar equalled the height of the hangings of the court, so He lived in complete harmony with the righteousness of God, eternally prepared and suited to meet all its requirements, no matter the cost.

In the acacia wood, of course, we see His perfect Manhood, Incorruptible spiritually, morally, physically, journeying on to Calvary. And in the bronze overlay we marvel as we see Him in infinite grace being made strong to endure the scourging and bruising of men, and the fierce, burning heat of the anger of God against sin. Nothing could turn Him back.

God had Himself foretold it all as He guided the writers of Psalm 22, of Isaiah 53 and all that the prophets had written concerning the sufferings of the Christ. The offerings at the bronze altar had enabled God in His forbearance to pass over sins for centuries. But all passing over of sins ceased at Calvary. There God went into the whole question of sin, once for all. He brought it out into the open. There the Son of God was so closely identified with the thing He loathed, that it is written, 'For He made Him who knew no sin to be sin for us, that we might become the righteousness of God in Him' (2 Cor.5:21).

So, for love's sake, He '... endured the cross, despising the shame' (Heb.12:2). Every morning the priest came in his linen garment, the garment which indicated holiness rather than 'glory and ... beauty' (Ex.28:2), and he took up the ashes to which the fire had consumed the burnt offering on the altar, and he placed them beside the altar. Then he put off the linen garments and put on others, doubtless those that spoke of the resurrection, and were for glory and beauty, and he carried the ashes outside the camp to a clean place.

In the tender shadows, God saw the rich man foretold in Isaiah 53:9 come with Nicodemus, with the mixture of myrrh and aloes. Gently taking down the body of Jesus, they laid it in the new tomb, wherein never man had lain. The work that the Father had given Him to do was finished to absolute divine satisfaction. The fires of divine judgement had, in the language of the types, burned the Victim to ashes. The atonement was complete.

But the altar stood high, foursquare, with bloodstained horns at each top corner. Here was the Christ for all to see, for people of all nations to receive, in His universal, resurrection power and authority to save. Well did Peter say, 'Therefore let all ... know assuredly that God has made this Jesus, whom you crucified, both Lord and Christ' (Acts 2:36).

During the long history of the bronze altar the staves were in use but briefly. Over forty times during their stay in the wilderness, Israel struck camp, journeyed and then pitched, all at the commandment of the Lord (Num.33:1-49). For each of these journeys the bronze altar was wrapped in a purple cloth, covered with badger skins, the staves were put in, then Levites of the family of Kohath carried it on their shoulders. Men linked in service carried the altar of God proudly, high on their shoulders. The Lord said to Ananias regarding Saul of Tarsus, '... he is a chosen vessel of Mine to bear My name' (Acts 9:15).

Paul, with his incisive mind, his brilliant intellect, his unrivalled knowledge of the Old Testament Scriptures, could easily have struck out on his own, impatient with men of lesser calibre. But it became the dedication of Paul's life to bear the Name of the glorified Lord Jesus Christ to men, in a fellowship of service with his brethren in the churches of God. Personal witness is basic to all Christian life. But in the New Testament, disciples are seen in a fellowship of assemblies, having fellowship together in royal priesthood service, taking the glad tidings of the Lord Jesus to the people. Thus, as a royal priesthood the people of God today have a ministry man-ward, just as Israel's priests served on behalf of others at the bronze altar outside in the court.

The days of the bronze altar are over. Its flow of blood has ceased. Its endless offering of sacrifice had never been able to make the worshipper perfect. It had stood as a great monument to the remembrance of sin. But by glorious contrast, the Lord Jesus offered one sacrifice for sins forever, sat down at the right hand of God, ... by one offering He has perfected forever those who are being sanctified' (Heb.10:12,14).

Our joy is the continual remembrance of Him (1 Cor.11:24,25). This brings us to one final point in relation to the bronze altar with its clear message for us today. It was on the fire taken from the altar that the incense was laid which perfumed the Holy Place every morning and every evening and the Most Holy Place on the great Day of Atonement. This was another reason why the fire on the altar had never to go out. The people of God today are called to a continual service of fragrant prayer and worship in the house of God and the basis of all this is a constant heartwarming appreciation of the Lord Jesus.

The Spirit of God laid down a basic principle when He led David, in other circumstances, to write, 'My heart was hot within me; while I was musing, the fire burned. Then I spoke with my tongue' (Ps.39:3). To some there may be a temptation to be present at the assembly gatherings for prayer and worship and, without anything particular in mind, just key into the thoughts of others.

But David interpreted the shadow in a better way. As he mused his heart was stirred and, thus compelled, he spoke. David was musing about injustice, but we muse about the Justifier. It is very well pleasing to the Lord when as disciples we spend time over the Word, meditating on the excellencies of Him who called us out of darkness into His marvellous light, until our hearts burn in appreciation and then in the midst of the assembly we speak, or inwardly express, the things we have made touching the King (Ps.45:1).

So we have traced briefly how the sinner in search of God comes by way of Christ in His life at the gate of the court, and at the altar sees Christ the Lamb of God going into death for his sake. Just as the offerer in Israel laid his hand on the head of his sacrifice, confessed his sin and identified himself with the victim in its substitutionary death, so

> My faith would lay her hand
>
> On that dear Head of Thine,
>
> While like a penitent I stand,
>
> And there confess my sin.
>
> (I. Watts, HSS 142/RS 217)

Then, and only then, can the forgiven sinner pass on and become eligible for priestly service among the people of God in His house. Then only can he offer back his life to God as a living sacrifice (Rom.12:1), a dedication of life in appreciation of the Son of God who loved him, and gave Himself up for him (Gal.2:20), a yielded reciprocity.

CHAPTER 12: THE LAVER

Exodus 30:17-21; 38:8; 40:30

To the pious Israelite it was a moment of ecstatic joy when he came to the altar of God and met Him there in the court of His dwelling place. One of them put it this way, 'Oh, send out Your light and Your truth! Let them lead me; let them bring me to Your holy hill and to Your tabernacle. Then I will go to the altar of God, to God my exceeding joy' (Ps. 43:3,4). But, as we have seen, that was the limit of his access to the presence of God. Only the family of Aaron could go further, but it was instant death to do so without first washing at the laver, the place for ritual washing.

There were three articles of Tabernacle furniture that were wholly made of metal and had no acacia wood. One of these was the laver, wholly made of bronze. Two articles of furniture had no measurements laid down in the pattern shown to Moses. Again, one of these was the laver. Doubtless Moses had a clear picture in his mind as to the shape of the vessel, and its overall appearance in relation to the size of the other vessels. But in its construction, its size corresponded to the vision in a unique way.

There were certain '... serving women who assembled at the door of the tabernacle of meeting' (Ex.38:8). Since the Tabernacle was not yet constructed these may well have been the wise-hearted women who spun the blue and the purple, the scarlet and the fine linen; the women whose hearts were stirred up in wisdom to spin the goats' hair (Ex.35:25,26), and they may have brought their work to the private tent of meeting which Moses had, as referred to in Exodus 33:7. These serving women, however, brought also their bronze mirrors as a spontaneous personal contribution to the construction of the Tabernacle. They would be of great value to these women in their daily adornment, and as a mark of divine appreciation it was from these mirrors that Moses directed, doubtless by the Spirit, that the bronze laver be made.

Since the laver was essentially for the use of the priests, directions regarding it are not given to Moses till after the details of the sanctification of the priesthood, the altar of incense and the atonement money have all been dealt with. There is less written as to its specification and construction than of any other vessel, neither is any subsequent specific reference made to it in Scripture, nor even in connection with the covering of the sacred vessels when Israel was on the march. It has clearly one basic but profound teaching attached to it.

The laver is generally thought to have been circular in plan, due no doubt to the idea of roundness in the root meaning of the word. It was made of bronze and had a bronze base. It was placed between the bronze altar and the door of the tent of meeting. It was filled with water, and the priests washed at it, not in it. In all probability the actual washing took place at the base. Thus, the water in the laver would never be defiled.

It was exclusively for the use of the priests. No priestly service was conducted at it but none could be conducted without it. Originally the priesthood consisted of Aaron and his four sons. Sadly two of them, Nadab and Abihu, who had seen '... God, and they ate and drank' in His presence on Sinai (Ex.24:11) and had each gone through the solemn ritual of sanctification for ministry in the priest's office (Ex.28,29), fell into immediate trespass in the holy things and '... died before the LORD' (Lev.10:2). So the priesthood of Israel virtually began with three men Aaron, Eleazar and Ithamar.

The nation of Israel was by divine definition '... a kingdom of priests' (Ex.19:6), or as expressed in the Septuagint (the Greek version of the Old Testament): '... a royal priesthood'. But every person in Israel was not a priest in the priesthood when God gave Moses the pattern of the

Tabernacle and its services He stipulated on Sinai that Aaron and his sons should be appointed priests on behalf of the nation. And the marvel is that while God was outlining to Moses the manner of their appointment, Aaron himself was busily engaged at the foot of the mountain making a golden calf for the people to worship, in an intolerable association with a feast to the Lord. So, as Moses cast down the stones, God had to begin not only with a broken law, but also an erring priesthood.

When the erection of the Tabernacle was completed, on the first day of the first month of the second year; when the structure and all its furniture had been anointed with the holy oil, then Moses washed Aaron and his sons at the laver, put on them the holy garments and anointed them to set them apart to God for their priestly service.

The whole objective in their being hallowed, sanctified, set apart for God in this way was that they might take up the work of ministry in the service of God related to His dwelling place. Thereafter it was the priests' own responsibility to 'wash their hands and their feet in water from it. When they go into the tabernacle of meeting, or when they come near the altar to minister, to burn an offering made by fire to the LORD, they shall wash with water, lest they die. So they shall wash their hands and their feet, lest they die. And it shall be a statute forever to them - to him and his descendants throughout their generations' (Ex.30:19-21). So the warning was given twice for powerful emphasis, '... lest they die'.

The bronze altar was for the judgement of sin in the individual. The bronze laver was for the cleansing of defilement in the priests of Israel's priesthood, as they carried out the services of the house of God. They were initially washed by Moses in the day when they were hallowed to minister; thereafter they were responsible to wash their own hands and feet before serving. The typical teaching of the laver has therefore in view the initial and daily cleansing of those who today are priests in the holy and royal priesthood spoken of in 1 Peter 2:5,9; who are attending on the services of the spiritual house of God of 1 Peter 2:5; whose consciences have been cleansed from dead works so that they might serve the living God in the greater and more perfect Tabernacle (Heb.9:14).

In the writer's understanding, all believers in the Lord Jesus Christ are viewed as priests, available for the priesthood service. Ephesians 5:25,26 says that '... Christ also loved the church and gave Himself for her, that He might sanctify and cleanse her with the washing of water by the word'. This sanctifying of the Church by Christ is His setting of it apart so that there might be available to all its members a place of service with other members in the priesthood. To all members of the Church, which is His Body, is presented in Scripture the opportunity of a place in the spiritual house of God, a subject that will be developed in subsequent chapters. For these, as for all believers, there is a vital present-day truth in the laver.

We have already noted that there was no acacia wood in the laver, so that the humanity of the Lord Jesus cannot be in view. It was made entirely of bronze, which we have already associated in our minds with durability, strength and judgement. What in the Scriptures has all these qualities and stands related also to the cleansing of defilement? The psalmist seems to answer the question by asking another: 'How can a young man cleanse his way? By taking heed according to Your word' (Ps.119:9).

This is supported by the two references to the word laver in the New Testament. The references are in the original Greek, not in the text. First there is the expression already referred to in Ephesians 5:26, '... the washing (laver) of water by the word'. Then in Titus 3:5 '... the washing (laver) of regeneration', which is of course the Word of God (1 Pet.1:23). To an exercised heart today nothing is so penetrating as the Scriptures. David wrote, 'Search me, O God, and know my heart; try me, and know my anxieties' (Ps.139:23). And the New Testament echoes, 'For the word of God is living and powerful, and sharper than any two-edged sword ... a discerner of the thoughts and intents of the heart' (Heb.4:12).

The washing of Israel's priests at the laver, first done to them by Moses and then done by themselves continually, finds a choice illustration in the upper room scene in John 13. John presents the Lord Jesus there as the eternal Son, knowing perfectly that shortly He would leave the world to return to the Father. With Him were the men He loved, who had stood by Him in all His trials. In the room the good-man of the house had left the basin of water and the towel for the customary freshening of the guests' feet. But no one had taken the opportunity. Indeed no man is recorded as ever washing the Lord's feet. Only women did that, with the affectionate touch. To them, they were the beautiful feet of Isaiah 52:7. So in a physical demonstration of the spiritual stoop of Philippians 2:1-8, the Lord and Master washed and wiped the feet of all the disciples present.

Peter protested, 'You shall never wash my feet!' (John 13:8, using the Greek word niptō, meaning the washing of a part of the body). The Lord used the same word in reply: 'If I do not wash you, you have no part with Me'. He did not say 'no relationship with Me'; but rather no fellowship or communion. Whereupon Peter asked that, if such were the case, his hands and his head might be washed also. This brought the memorable response, 'He who is bathed needs only to wash his feet, but is completely clean' (John 13:10).

Here, 'bathed' is the Greek word louō, meaning to wash the whole body and 'wash' simply niptō as before. Of the two washings in the New Testament, one is done by the Lord at conversion at the laver of regeneration. As a result of this we are clean every whit in the imputed righteousness of Christ. The new man thus created never sins: 'he cannot sin, because he has been born of God' (1 John 3:9).

The second washing is done by ourselves, the washing of our own feet, that is the cleansing of our own ways at the laver of the Word, as we are daily conscious of the defilements of flesh and spirit; these weaknesses in the old nature which trouble us.

These defilements in our walk affect our fellowship with the Lord and with one another; they harm our testimony; they silence us in the sanctuary; they weaken us before men. So we come continually to the Lord in confession of waywardness, as corrected by the Word, and thus continually cleanse our ways in priestly service. Many a disciple has failed in the vital matter of cleansing away the defilements of the journey, ignoring the solemn principle '... lest they die'. Spiritual death has ensued. The need for personal confession and cleansing from defilement before entering on any form of priestly exercise will always remain vital. In the Church of God in Corinth some ceased to examine themselves before participating in the Remembrance. This led to eating and drinking judgement to themselves, then they became weak and sick and many slept (i.e., died). So there are some matters in priestly service that we cannot afford to ignore.

Two other points arise here. The first is that the Lord Jesus has taught us in John 13 to wash our feet - not our hands. This makes us reflect on the fact that we live in the dispensation of the Spirit, and serve God in His spiritual house. Israel's priests served in a material house. As a consequence they handled physical things that related to the various aspects of service; the altar with its sacrifices, the table with its bread, the lampstand with its oil, to mention a few. So as they went into the sanctuary to trim the lamps at the hour of the morning sacrifice, their hands stained from service at the altar and their feet soiled from the sandy desert floor, they would wash their hands and feet. But in the spiritual house God's priests wash, spiritually, their feet only, that is their ways, otherwise they can have no part with Him. Only washed, undefiled feet can walk with Him in a sharing fellowship of service.

The second point is that the Lord Jesus taught us in John 13 to wash one another's feet. This, of course, was done by some in a physical sense, as, for example, the well reported sisters of 1 Timothy 5:10 who had '... washed the saints' feet'. But there is an obligation on us all by our Master's example that by the gentle ministry of the Word we should help to soothe the weary feet of fellow-saints, to help them to adjust if they are beginning to turn out of the way. Peter, who never forgot that night, had later a word to describe the operation. He wrote, 'Yes, all of you be submissive to one another, and be clothed with humility, for "God resists the proud, but gives grace to the humble" (1 Pet.5:5).

It would be interesting to know whether the priest, as he washed, could see himself reflected darkly in the sides of the laver, since it was made from brightly polished mirrors which formerly had reflected the gifting women in their adornment. One thing is certain that in the mirror of our laver, 'we all, with unveiled face, beholding as in a mirror the glory of the Lord, are being transformed into the same image from glory to glory, just as by the Spirit of the Lord' (2 Cor.3:18). In the Word we see not only our own defilements, but by contrast the personal glories and excellencies of the Lord. As we meditate on any one of them, it becomes in part at least absorbed into our lives and we become transformed into that same glory.

In a final reflection we note that in Revelation 4:6 and Revelation 15:2 there appears to be the heavenly substance of which the Tabernacle laver was the earthly shadow. It was a sea of glass like crystal, mingled with fire. On this sea stood 'those who have the victory over the beast, over his image and over his mark and over the number of his name ...'

They had harps of God and sang '... the song of Moses, the servant of God, and the song of the Lamb ...' (Rev.15:3). No more washing, nor need for cleansing, for the days of earthly defilement are over. No more the fires of persecution, no more tribulation, for the days of the beast are over. As we contemplate the glassy sea, the vast laver above, it seems to become to us the symbol of absolute purity in complete security.

"Search me, O God, and know my heart to-day;

Try me, O Saviour, know my thoughts, I pray;

See if there be some wicked way in me:

Cleanse me from every sin, and set me free."

(E.J. Orr, GS 213)

CHAPTER 13: THE TABERNACLE CURTAIN

Exodus 26:1-6; 36:8-13

As the hour of the morning sacrifice approached, the officiating priests would wash at the laver. Certain of them would then go to the bronze altar to attend to the offering of the lamb, with its meal offering and accompanying oil and wine. Others would proceed to the Tabernacle to render service within at the golden lampstand and the golden altar of incense. The Tabernacle structure may not have appeared particularly attractive to the priests as they drew near. But when they passed through the door of the tent of meeting the sight was deeply impressive. Outside the vessels were of bronze and for judgement, but here inside they were of pure gold for glory. On either side were the golden boards, overhead was the beautiful curtain of rich embroidered work, and ahead was the veil. Beyond that dwelt God between the cherubim, above the mercy seat, over the ark of the covenant. The structure was God's house. In it everything said, glory. It was the glory of holiness. The symbolic cherubim were to be seen everywhere.

It all began with the invitation of God to Israel, following their constitution as His people at Sinai, '... let them make Me a sanctuary, that I may dwell among them' (Ex.25:8). In those choice days of Israel's first love, the love of her espousals to and by God, the people were so stirred that they came to Moses with their freewill offerings of every type of material required for the building of the sanctuary. Exodus 35:20-36:7 tells the fascinating story and the reader will greatly profit by perusing it.

No amount of piled up material, however willingly given, could have been regarded as God's house; just as today no number of children of God, however enthusiastic they may be, can form God's spiritual house

THE PARABLE OF THE TABERNACLE 53

unless they are built together according to the divine pattern. So the Lord filled two men with His Spirit, Bezalel of the tribe of Judah, and Aholiab of the tribe of Dan, in such a way that they had a unique capacity not only to know how every intricate part of the Tabernacle and its furniture should be made, of whatever material, but also they had the gift of imparting that knowledge to others. Thus, in due course, when everything was in place according to the pattern showed to Moses on the mount, God took up His abode in His sanctuary in the midst of His people.

The Tabernacle itself was one beautifully made curtain, measuring twenty-eight cubits long by forty cubits broad. Wise-hearted women spun with their hands the fine linen in the three colours, and from this material wise-hearted men made ten curtains, the cherubim being all inwrought. They were all made from the same '... fine woven linen, and blue, purple, and scarlet thread; with artistic designs of cherubim you shall weave them' (Ex.26:1).

They each had the same measurement, twenty-eight cubits long by four cubits broad. First they coupled five of the curtains together, we are not told in what way. Then they coupled the other five curtains together. Along the one edge of each set of five coupled curtains they put loops of blue. They then linked the fifty loops of blue which were opposite the one to the other with fifty clasps of gold. As a consequence '... it became one tabernacle'. (Ex.36:13 KJV).

It was a composite unity of ten individual, comparable curtains, coupled and clasped. The size of the structure was determined by the number and size of the supporting boards, and measured thirty cubits long, ten cubits broad and ten cubits high. This meant that the curtain of forty cubits breadth hung along the full thirty cubits length of the structure and the remaining ten cubits hung down to the ground at the back. The curtain, twenty-eight cubits in length, had to hang over the thirty cubits, that is the ten cubits height on both sides and the ten cubits width. This meant that it was two cubits short, so that the curtain came down to one cubit from the ground along both sides.

Since this one curtain formed the Tabernacle, God's house where He dwelt, God's sanctuary where He was worshipped, we are now at one of the most vital points in our study and it is good that we get as close as we can to the mind of the Spirit in our understanding of its teaching for today. For example, many teachers have seen in this Tabernacle a foreshadowing of the Lord Jesus Christ, in those great days when He '... dwelt (Greek, tabernacled) among us' (John 1:14) In Him was a detailed correspondence to the blue, the purple, the scarlet, the fine linen thread. 'For in Him dwells all the fullness of the Godhead bodily' (Col.2:9) and John wrote, '... we beheld His glory' (John 1:14). With this we are in complete agreement. But this cannot be the main teaching of the Tabernacle. The whole point about the Tabernacle was that it presented God as dwelling among a covenanted people. It must therefore have foreshadowed principles on the basis of which God would one day dwell in a spiritual house among another covenanted people. Besides, God dwelling in this house was conditional on Israel's obedience and compliance with their part of the covenant of Sinai. All this is seen culminating in the condemnation of Matthew 23:38, 'See! Your house is left to you desolate'. This could never have been true of the Son of God in His Manhood.

Others have taught that the Tabernacle prefigures the Church, which is His Body. But nowhere in the New Testament is that Church presented as constituting either the house or temple of God. The house and the temple are conditional, in God's recognition of them, on obedience and holding fast to the teaching of the Lord, as expressed in such portions as 1 Corinthians 3:16,17; Hebrews 3:6; 1 Peter 4:17. Furthermore, to be specific, what is there in the Church the Body that would find any typical expression in the Tabernacle curtain?

In what way then did the ten curtains, coupled and clasped into one, foreshadow the house of God in New Testament times? This is a spiritual house, composed of disciples of the Lord Jesus Christ; persons who, following acceptance of Christ as Saviour, have acknowledged His lordship in their baptism and been added to a church of God. How this was brought about in the case of those in the Church of God in Jerusalem is outlined in Acts 2:41,42 and subsequent chapters; and in Corinth in Acts 18:8, for example. Such persons are seen foreshadowed in the fine linen thread, the blue, purple, scarlet and the embroidered cherubim. We have already indicated in chapter 6, that when we find these materials in this order what is in view is evidently persons taking on the likeness of Christ as distinct from the order in which the blue comes first where clearly the Lord Jesus Christ is Himself in view, '... which thing is true in Him and in you' (1 John 2:8).

Thus, the three screens speak of the Lord Jesus and the curtains speak of disciples who are seeking to reflect His glories. In each of the ten curtains we see foreshadowed a church of God. These churches are referred to in the New Testament as: churches of God (1 Thess.2:14), churches of Christ (Rom.16:16), churches of the saints (1 Cor.14:33).

It has been pointed out that they are churches of God as to their constitution, churches of the saints as to their composition and churches of Christ as to their character. They are composed of disciples who have been given the righteousness of Christ at conversion and are to work out a corresponding righteousness in their lives.

In the blue we are reminded of their heavenly calling and the heavenly home on which their affections are to be set. In the purple we contemplate disciples as part of a royal priesthood, all of them (like Gideon's brothers] resembling the children of a King. In the scarlet they are earnestly seeking to reflect in service the lowly mind of Christ. In the inwrought cherubim there is a constant, powerful reminder to disciples in the house of God that it is written, 'Be holy, for I am holy' (1 Pet.1:16); that God's '... holy priesthood' (1 Pet.2:5) and '... holy nation' (1 Pet.2:9) who minister the holy things' (1 Cor.9:13) are to be holy women and men who lift up '... holy hands' (1 Tim.2:8).

The ten curtains were not only made from the same material but they all had exactly the same measurements. The uniformity of teaching (1 Cor.4:17) and of practice (1 Cor.11:16; 14:33) in the New Testament churches was an interesting development and is a profitable study. It was the logical outcome of the great initiating commission of the Lord in Matthew 28:19,20, 'Go therefore and make disciples of all the nations, baptizing them ... teaching them to observe all things that I have commanded you.'

When disciples had been made and baptized they were formed into units of divine testimony known as churches of God, so that together in assembly they might be taught the observance of all the Lord's commandments. Paul describes the operation in Romans 6:17 as '... that form of doctrine to which you were delivered', or that mould of teaching into which they were poured. All the churches were together in their understanding of the Faith and united in the way they gave effect to it.

We noted that the first set of five curtains were all coupled together. The Hebrew word here translated coupled is used elsewhere in the Old Testament. For example in Psalm 94:20 it says, 'Shall the throne of iniquity, which devises evil by law, have fellowship with You?' Here the thought is of fellowship with. Again, in Psalm 122:3, 'Jerusalem is built as a city that is compact together'. Here the thought is compact together. Indeed in the Septuagint this verse is rendered, '... a city whose fellowship is complete'. This completeness was beautifully seen when the golden clasps bound the two sets of five curtains into one Tabernacle.

It was a remarkable foreshadowing of the New Testament dwelling place. The churches of God were not in any sense autonomous units of testimony, all standing in independence, answerable only to the Lord. Rather, they were linked together in an ever-widening fellowship of assemblies. The illustrative table that follows, a slightly shortened version of Dr. C. M. Luxmoore's original[5], indicates the principle. Each church of God, viewed as a building in, for example, 1 Corinthians 3:9, was '... compact together' with the other churches of God. They were an integrated movement, the fellowship of which was everywhere complete. '... In whom the whole building, being fitted together, grows into a holy temple in the Lord', is how the Spirit describes it in Ephesians 2:21. So the original Church of God in Jerusalem grew to become the church throughout all Judea and Galilee and Samaria (Acts 9:31). The work spread in unity. Or as one has put it in other circumstances, 'In harmony small things grow'.

Assembly	Early reference	Grouped in Roman Province of	Province reference	Wider groupings references	
Jerusalem	Acts 2	Judea	1 Thess. 2:14 Gal. 1:22		
Lydda	Acts 9				
Sharon	Acts 9			Acts 9:3	
Joppa	Acts 9				
Samaria	Acts 8	Samaria			
Caesarea	Acts 21				
Lystra	Acts 14	Galatia	Gal. 1:2		
Derbe	Acts 14		1 Cor. 16:1		
Iconium	Acts 14				
Antioch	Acts 14				
Ephesus	Acts 18	Asia	1 Cor. 16:19		John 17:11,20-23
Smyrna	Rev. 2		Rev. 1:11		1 Cor. 1:9
Pergamum	Rev. 2			1 Pet. 1:1	Eph. 2:21
Thyatira	Rev. 2				1 Pet. 2:5
Sardis	Rev. 3				
Philadelphia	Rev. 3				
Laodicea	Col. 4				
Colossae	Col. 1				
Philippi	Acts 16	Macedonia	2 Cor. 8:1		
Thessalonica	Acts 17				
Beroea	Acts 17				
Corinth	Acts 18	Achaia	2 Cor. 1:1		
Cenchrea	Rom. 16				

When, in due course, the financial need of the churches of God in Judea became known to the churches of Macedonia (2 Cor.8:1), there was an immediate response from one grouping of churches to another; for they were in the same fellowship of assemblies, 'the fellowship of His Son, Jesus Christ our Lord' (1 Cor.1:9). The New Testament house of God is one, whatever the number of churches of God composing it,

THE PARABLE OF THE TABERNACLE

bound together by the golden clasps of a divine teaching, even the faith of our Lord Jesus Christ, once for all delivered to the saints (Jude 3). This we believe to be the pattern for collective testimony shown to the apostles for our instruction throughout this dispensation. In strict accordance with it we must build for God without deviation. The teaching of Sinai still held good in Malachi 4:4, 'Remember the Law of Moses, My servant'. As then, so now; only He who gives the teaching can recall it.

'Tis precious too, O God,

Thine eye should look upon

Thy scattered children here

United into one.

Lord, may Thy word for ever be

Our guide to perfect unity.

Grant that more perfectly

Thy will may be expressed,

That gathered saints may show

The way of truth is best.

So mid this discord men may see

Divinely ordered unity.

(C. Belton, PHSS 409)

CHAPTER 14: THE CURTAIN OF GOATS' HAIR

Exodus 26:7-13; 36:14-18

Eleven curtains of goats' hair were placed over the Tabernacle and, like it, they were coupled together into one. Each goats' hair curtain was thirty cubits in length and four cubits in breadth. Five were coupled together, then fifty loops of unspecified material were placed down the outside edge. The other six were similarly coupled and fifty loops placed in position. Fifty clasps of bronze then joined the opposite loops '... that it might be one' (Ex.36:18). There was therefore a tent of eleven curtains coupled together, measuring overall thirty by forty-four cubits, covering the Tabernacle of ten curtains coupled together measuring twenty-eight by forty cubits.

The covering tent came right down and touched the ground on the north and south sides, whereas the Tabernacle curtain was one cubit short on both sides. Further, it only required forty cubits to cover the Tabernacle curtain from the top of the door in the east, right along to the western end and down to the ground; so that one curtain of four cubits was in excess. This curtain was to be doubled over in the forefront of the tent. In other words, it hung down at the top of the door and was visible for all to see. When it says that '... the half curtain that remains, shall hang over the back of the tabernacle' (Ex.26:12), this was a half of the five curtains coupled together, or a breadth of ten cubits, exactly the backdrop to the ground on the west side. Once again we note that '... all the women whose hearts stirred with wisdom spun yarn of goats' hair' (Ex.35:26). There is no word 'hair' in the original, but since spinning was involved it can be safely assumed. The goat was black in colour (compare Song of Songs 1:5; 6:5).

This tent was frequently referred to as the tent of meeting, but this is not to be confused with the personal tent of Moses, similarly named in Exodus 33:7. This tent was placed outside the camp when the people sinned grievously in the idolatry of the golden calf. Those who sought the Lord had to leave what was a defiled camp and go to meet Moses in a tent pitched afar off. The Tabernacle and its tent of meeting had not at that time been constructed.

The word 'meeting', in the tent of meeting, carries the thought of meeting by appointment and this was an essential feature of the structure. In the Tabernacle God dwelt with His people. In the tent of meeting His people came representatively to meet with Him. The tent therefore touched the ground and the priests of Israel only came into the tent at prescribed times and for specific purposes.

It would be difficult to dissociate the goat from the Day of Atonement, and thus, typically, the goat from atonement generally. This great basic truth was pre-eminently displayed in the goats' hair curtain hanging down over the entrance to the Tabernacle. It was there for all to see, the dwelling of God among His people rested on the atonement. Similarly, the whole arrangement for men meeting with God was based on the atonement.

The Day of Atonement occurred on one day only in the year. But, as the Israelite came to the bronze altar and ahead of him saw the single goats' hair curtain over the entrance to the Tabernacle, black against the brilliant sky, he may well have had frequent meditation on the need for atonement and reconciliation to God by means of the altar.

For ourselves, our minds go immediately to the glorious Person of the Lord Jesus Christ, who came not to preach the atonement but to effect it at Calvary. Till then God had, in His forbearance, passed over the sins done aforetime by His people. But all passing over of sin ceased at Calvary. On that dark afternoon the eternal Son in His Manhood became answerable to God for the sin of Adam transmitted to his posterity, and additionally for all the sins of all who would accept Him as their substitute Saviour. 'For He made Him who knew no sin to be sin for us, that we might become the righteousness of God in Him' (2 Cor.5:21).

But in the pattern on the mount, so similar was the description of the construction of the Tabernacle curtain and the curtain of the tent of meeting that we cannot fail to see we are here considering in the type two different aspects of the same truth. Speaking to the elders of the Church of God in Ephesus, Paul said, 'Therefore take heed ... to shepherd (feed) the church of God which He purchased with His own blood' (Acts 20:28).

That is, God had acquired it with the blood of His own Son. It took the death of the Son of God to bring into existence churches of God. Here, in the tent of goats' hair, these churches are seen coupled together in relation to the great atonement and the bronze clasps make it clear that they are bound together by principles of discipline and judgement.

Peter wrote that the time had come for judgement to begin at the house of God. Paul described in 2 Thessalonians 1:5 how that the righteous judgement of God stood related to the churches and kingdom of God. The divine principle is that the Lord will judge His people. This reacts on the individual disciple who should have a keen sense of self-examination with a view to confession of waywardness to the Lord and to others also if such should be involved.

One principle is outlined in Matthew 5:23,24. If the disciple becomes conscious of having wronged his brother he should go immediately to him and thus, by reconciliation, live in the enjoyment of the greater reconciliation into which Christ's atonement has brought him. Again in Matthew 18:15-17 the principle is laid down by the Lord that if a brother is sinned against by another, then he should go to him privately with a view to reconciliation. But should this fail, the matter is too

THE PARABLE OF THE TABERNACLE 63

important to be allowed to rest and witnesses must be brought in and finally, if necessary, the church has to decide. So great atonement demands reconciled lives among God's people.

In difficult matters it is the responsibility of overseers to enquire into all relevant details so that guidance may be given to the saints as to the course of action to be pursued. The bronze clasps were in the same unity as the curtains and unity in oversight is essential if the people of God are to be maintained in harmony. For this reason the divine principle in the New Testament is that there should be a plurality of elders in every church (see Acts 14:23; Tit.1:5-9). In addition, these elders should act in fellowship with their fellow-elders in a wider circle (see Acts 11:29,30; 15:1-29). Just as the churches were in a fellowship of assemblies, so the elders stood collectively related to that fellowship. Israel was a fellowship of tribes, but the New Testament people of God was and is a fellowship of assemblies. So, in the new Israel of God, the responsibilities of elders widened out from a purely local care to a responsibility as wide as the holy nation, as was the case in other circumstances with the elders of Israel.

In connection with the tent of meeting, the Lord Jesus laid down in practice an early principle in Acts 1:4, 'And being assembled together with them ...' This has given character to the dispensation. Disciples are enjoined to gather together to engage in the collective service of the house of God. This is facilitated by the forethought of God in legislating for local churches of God, so that, for example, Paul says in 1 Corinthians 11:18, 'when you come together as a church'.

Again it is negatively expressed in Hebrews 10:25, '... not forsaking the assembling of ourselves together, as is the manner of some'. The Lord's people are appointed a holy priesthood and so they are invited to draw near on specific occasions for the breaking of the bread and the attendant service of worship in the heavenly sanctuary (Acts 2:42;

1 Cor.11:23-32; Heb.10:19-22). Also they are called for the prayers (Acts 2:42; 12:5; Heb.4:14-16) besides, of course, at other times of collective prayer related to their royal priesthood service. Each time we gather in the assembly to draw near in some aspect of divine service, it is a salutary thought to remember - I am going to meet with God.

The specific reference by the Spirit to the part the women played in spinning the goats' hair calls for a word of appreciation of the notable, often secret, service that so many beloved sisters render in the service of God today. We select for reference the ministry of:

- the family - so beautifully exemplified in Lois and Eunice,
- the open home - so well depicted in the life of Priscilla,
- the assembly activities - so excellently carried on by Euodia and Syntyche,
- the large heart - so clearly envisaged in the sisters of 1 Timothy 5:10.

May the Lord greatly recompense our beloved sisters and greatly increase to us their number.

CHAPTER 15: RAM SKINS DYED RED

Exodus 26:14; 36:19

Over the tent of meeting was first placed a covering of ram skins dyed red. This was doubtless a protective covering against the elements, whether the strong rays of the sun or the wind and the rain. No account is given of how it was made from the individual skins. The word ram comes from a root meaning to twist, as, to provide strength, strands of thread would be twisted. That the ram indicated strength is seen in the vision in Daniel 8:3,4. It was used in various offerings, but most will associate it with the consecration of the priests in Exodus 29 and Leviticus 8. It was the skins of rams that provided the leather covering. These were dyed red. There is no word for dyed in the Hebrew text but the translators have naturally understood that the skins were not always red. They were made red. The Hebrew word used here for red indicates the showing of red in the face as when a person flushes or blushes.

We have noted briefly in the two previous chapters some precious truths connected with the churches of God in this present period of grace. These truths have to be protected today as much as the Tabernacle curtains in Israel's day. They have to be defended against the biting winds of false doctrine and the hot scorn of cynicism. They have even to be upheld faithfully in the face of opposition from godly Christians, many of them well known to us and much loved by us, who maintain that there is nothing of a composite nature for God presented in the New Testament beyond the Church which is His Body - that there is no such thing as the house or temple of God separate and distinct from the Church the Body.

The whole counsel of God in connection with His house, as to doctrine, rule and conduct, is to be protected by an unlimited number of consecrated disciples (just as there were no measurements to the ram skin covering). The supreme example in Scripture of absolute consecration to the will of God is, of course, the Lord Jesus Christ. He was the Ram prefigured in Genesis 22:13: caught in the thicket by its horns. In the days of His flesh He had His own will but it was entirely surrendered to the will of His God and Father. There could be no greater expression of this than the 'nevertheless' of Luke 22:42. His was a consecration to the point of death, even the death of the Cross. From Him all consecrated disciples have taken character.

There was a powerfully symbolic completeness about the application of the blood of the ram of consecration to the priests in Israel. It was placed on the tip of the right ear, on the thumb of the right hand, and the great toe of the right foot. It was the consecration of the whole man to the service of God. The word consecration means, literally, to fill the hand. God was entrusting to the hands of these priests the maintenance of His service as a precious thing to be guarded. Then when the parts of the ram were prepared for the altar, Moses first laid them on the hands of each individual priest so that he might be made to feel the weight of his consecration.

As consecrated disciples take character from their dedicated Master, they feel the weight of responsibility affecting them in all their faculties and ways. Disciples like these will live their lives and, if need be, give their lives to protect the truths of God's spiritual house from the adversary. It was not long until persecution broke out on the early Christians; bonds and imprisonments, the spoiling of their possessions, accepted with all joy in the Holy Spirit. Then came the martyrdom of Stephen and James and 'Antipas was My faithful martyr' (Rev.2:13).

It is written of Paul: 'For I am already being poured out' (2 Tim.4:6); of Priscilla and Aquila: '... who risked their own necks for my life' (Rom.16:4); of Epaphroditus: '... he came close to death, not regarding his life' (Phil.2:30). Skin speaks of sacrifice. John the Baptist had a leather waistband. He was banded with sacrifice.

In the shadow of the ram skins dyed red, we have no difficulty in seeing disciples banded with sacrifice; consecrated, strong for the defence of the truth of God. But the red was a flushing, blushing red. Many a young ram skin has begun his consecrated life this way; a faltering, stammering confession, very self-consciously given. But it was a start and step by step the Spirit of God became increasingly his great Enabler, till he became a stalwart defender of the faith. Nor should we forget that the ram skin covering was not normally seen by the observer. It was covered by the badger skins. And much of the consecrated service of dedicated disciples of the Lord Jesus is carried out in the secret of the yielded life, with only the Lord able to appreciate and assess.

One of David's mighty warriors was Hurai of the brooks of Gaash (1 Chr.11:26,32). In the Hebrew root from which Hurai is derived is the thought 'to grow pale'. Gaash means 'quaking'. Many a quaking, pale-faced, hesitant disciple has, by the Lord's help, taken his stand; struck out for Him; and done exploits in the kingdom of God. The writer will not readily forget a young Indian disciple in Madras coming to him in the early morning after a public address on this subject the evening before. Earnestly and longingly he said, 'I would like to be a young ram skin dyed red'. Reader, would you?

> "No wound? No scar?
>
> Yet, as the Master shall the servant be,
>
> And pierced are the feet that follow Me;
>
> But thine are whole: can he have followed far
>
> Who has nor wound nor scar?"

(Amy Carmichael)

CHAPTER 16: SEALSKINS OR BADGER SKINS

Exodus 26:14; 36:19

This was the outer covering for the curtains. Again we are neither given measurements nor told how they pieced the skins together. Indeed there is uncertainty as to the precise nature of the material from which this covering was made. The AV/NKJV has badger skins; the RV sealskins; other translators, porpoise skins or goat skins. Dr. Strong, in his Exhaustive Concordance of the Bible, indicates an animal with fur (OT:8476), which might support the KJV/NKJV.

Such skins were also used as an inner covering for the ark of the covenant when the nation was on the march; and as an outer covering for the table of showbread, the lampstand, the golden altar, the bronze altar and '... all the utensils of service' (Num. 4:12). The word is only elsewhere used in Scripture in Ezekiel 16:10, 'I ... gave you sandals of badger skin (RV sealskin)'. It was clearly then a hard-wearing skin, and in the covering, the skins probably retained the animals' fur.

The outer appearance of the Tabernacle was drab compared to the beauty of the Tabernacle curtain as seen from the inside. Many have seen in this a foreshadowing of how the Lord Jesus appeared to the people of Israel, and to the vast numbers of the nations of the world ever since. With this is associated such scriptures as Isaiah 53:2, 'He has no form or comeliness; and when we see Him, there is no beauty that we should desire Him'.

This was not a question of physical form or attractiveness. How could the sinless One have been anything other than perfect in His appearance? But Israel was looking for a Messiah who would come in power and, with banners marching high, throw off the Roman yoke. They saw no attractiveness in a lowly Messiah who was on His way to Calvary to make the atonement, and settle for ever the question of sin.

With the man in the street today there is still something unattractive about the Lord Jesus in His lowly Manhood, even though He was accomplishing for the human family what in all the eons of time they could never have accomplished for themselves. When here He was 'The stone which the builders rejected' (Ps.118:22; 1 Pet.2:7).

The builders were the leaders of Israel. He did not fit into any of their schemes. Nor does He conform to the material targets at which men aim today. Thus, the moral beauties and spiritual excellencies of the Son of God, the everlasting Lover of our unworthy race, the great substitutionary sacrifice for the whole world if they will but receive Him, all go unobserved by the blinded children of men.

We must, however, remain faithful to the type and remember that it was the beauties of the Tabernacle curtain, God's house and dwelling place, which were hidden from the observer as he looked at the badger skins. What is foreshadowed in the type is basically the fact that it is the glories of the spiritual house of God, as expressed in the churches of God, which prove unattractive to the observer today. Certain truths are not popular and this is certainly one of them. The way is too narrow. But we recall the words of the late W.J. Lennox of Armagh, a leader among those who rediscovered the truth of the house and churches of God towards the end of the 19th century, 'The way may be narrow, but let us pack it thick!'

The fellowship of assemblies in a spiritual unity is one of the lovely gems among the truths of the New Testament. The Lord Jesus prayed that His disciples might all be one; that they might form one thing in unity. This was not the unity of 'the church, which is His body' (Eph.1:22,23). There was no need to pray for the unity in Christ of all those who in one Spirit are baptized into one Body. Against that

Church the gates of hell cannot prevail. It is beyond the reach of satanic attack. But the Lord prayed that the members of the Church which is His Body might be kept in a visible, composite unity which all the world might see and by reason of which men might believe.

It is a very lovely thing, and greatly to the glory of God, when disciples in churches of God can live together in a unitedly accepted understanding of the teaching and practice enjoined upon all believers by the Lord, under the guidance of a united elderhood, subjecting themselves one to another in the fear of Christ. On the other hand it is very sad to think that so many believers see no appealing beauty in something that is so pleasant to the Lord and to those who have seen the vision of the house of God for today.

God's word to Ezekiel regarding the house of Israel was, '... let them measure the pattern' (Ezek.43:10).

It may be that beloved fellow-believers, as they prayerfully consider what has been briefly set forward in connection with the typical teaching of the curtains and their coverings, will check with the Scriptures the accuracy of the teaching presented and it is our earnest, affectionate prayer that many will come into the glory of fellowship in the spiritual house of God.

CHAPTER 17: THE BOARDS, WITH THEIR SOCKETS, BARS AND RINGS

Exodus 26:15-30; 36:20-34

As we have seen, the Tabernacle, or dwelling place of God, was the composite curtain of fine linen thread, and blue and purple and scarlet. Immediately following the details of its manufacture the details of '... the boards of acacia wood' (for the Tabernacle) are given (Ex.26:15). These upright boards supported the curtain so that the boards were closely integrated into the Tabernacle structure and were essential to it. Without the boards the Tabernacle could not have been raised up (Ex.26:30).

The boards were made of acacia wood, standing up. The phrase standing upright' (Ex. 26:15) was interpreted by the rabbis '... to mean that the natural growth of the wood should be respected in aligning the boards, so that the root-end of the tree shall be near the ground and, the crest at the top'. Each board was ten cubits long and one and a half cubits broad. No reference is given to the thickness of the boards. If, however, the overall width of the structure was ten cubits (as we noted when dealing with the curtains), and the two strengthening boards were placed as indicated below, then the boards would be one half cubit thick.

At the foot of each board, and part of it, were two tenons, joined together. These were small projections which fitted into two sockets of silver. The Hebrew word translated tenon, means 'a hand'; so they were like two small hands gripping firmly down into the silver foundation. These sockets were thus the foundation on which each board rested. The entrance to the Tabernacle faced east. The north and south sides

THE PARABLE OF THE TABERNACLE 73

respectively comprised twenty boards, resting on forty silver sockets. On the west side there were six boards, resting on twelve sockets. In addition, on the west side there was a strengthening board at each corner, again resting on its two sockets. These corner boards were coupled or twinned (as the Hebrew word suggests - Strong's OT:8535] to the board alongside at the foot, and continued the whole length of the board to the top where they were ringed together. Altogether there were forty-eight boards resting on ninety-six sockets of silver.

When we refer to forty-eight boards and have in view single planks each ten cubits long, it should be pointed out that this is a matter on which there is diversity of thought and the various views merit study. Some have difficulty in envisaging acacia trees of sufficient height to produce boards of the prescribed length. Others feel that planks of this size would prove too heavy for transport when the nation was on the march. The most weighty objection is that of A.R.S. Kennedy (see Hastings' Dictionary of the Bible, IV p.659-662)[6].

Briefly, his argument is that the boards were not solid planks '... but frames comprised of two uprights, joined by cross-rails, somewhat like a ladder'. The reader may wish to give this matter further study. But for our present purpose we shall assume single boards as already referred to and rely on Jerome's fourth century comment on the lightness of the acacia wood and the fact that long planks could be cut from the tree - despite the comment by one writer recently on '... the usual idea of boards, as seen in well-meaning but possibly incorrect models'!

Doubtless to strengthen the structure, bars of acacia wood were provided. These were five bars on the north, south and west sides. The centre bar in the middle on each side was to '... pass through the midst of the boards from end to end' (Ex.26:28). The general view, followed here, is that there were four external parallel bars on each of the three sides, with a fifth unseen middle bar passing through the middle of all the boards from end to end. As strengthening bars, all five would doubtless go the full length, but emphasis is placed on the fact that the unseen bar did so. Others take the view that on each side there were two parallel lengths of bars, each one divided, thus giving a space between - a total of four bars and an external fifth bar lay central to these but continuous for the full length. The reason behind this may be the difficulty some have in so complicated an arrangement as the exact positioning of a hole in each board so that a bar could pass right through the middle. But it would be wrong to underestimate the profound skill of Spirit-taught Bezalel and Aholiab (Ex.35:30-35).

There were rings of gold on each side through which the four bars passed. Finally the boards and bars were overlaid with gold. When in due course '... the tabernacle was raised up' (Ex.40:17), the integration of the boards and the curtain is remarkably indicated in Exodus 40:18,19, 'So Moses raised up the tabernacle, fastened its sockets, set up its boards, put in its bars, and raised up its pillars. And he spread out the tent over the tabernacle and put the covering of the tent on top of it, as the LORD had commanded Moses'.

The boards supported the curtain in forming God's house. In the New Testament we see that God's present purpose is that individual disciples of the Lord Jesus Christ, standing together in testimony, form the churches of God, His spiritual house. The boards were from acacia trees, which had been once rooted elsewhere but were cut down and fashioned according to the pattern shown to Moses on the mount. Those who today own the Lordship of Christ were by nature children of wrath, just as the others; they were without Christ, alienated; they had no hope and were without God in the world (see Eph. 2:1-12). Then one day the gospel reached them. Wuest likens the operation of the furtherance of the gospel in Philippians 1:5 to wood cutters preceding progress of an army cutting road through a forest for advance[7]. So they were cut down in their natural standing to be fashioned anew in Christ. They were '... born again, not of corruptible seed but incorruptible, through the word of God which lives and abides forever' (1 Pet.1:23).

Thus, disciples came into the likeness of the Christ of the acacia wood. The boards were then overlaid with gold. The Lord Jesus gives to His disciples His own glory, even as He said, 'And the glory which You gave Me I have given them' (John 17:22). Thus, they become '... partakers of the divine nature' (2 Pet.1:4); not the very nature of God, but a nature which is divine in origin and character. The beauty of the boards was the appearance of golden glory with no trace of the acacia wood ever again showing. What a challenge this is to disciples who form God's house, that what is seen of them by others are the beauties of the new nature, dedicated disciples moulded into the likeness of Christ.

> "Like Him in all those lovely traits,
>
> Which in His lowly, earthly days
>
> So beautiful we see."
>
> (C.M. Luxmoore, PHSS 415)

Paul found out in due course that he had been separated from his mother's womb and called through God's grace so that He might reveal His Son in him (Gal.1:15,16). The life of Christ was to be unveiled in Paul so as to be visible for others to see. So Paul determined that, by the Spirit's help, Christ would live in him (Gal.2:20); be formed in him (as in Gal. 4:19); and be magnified in him (Phil.1:20). For Paul it was, no longer I but Christ.

Trees cut down became boards standing up. When the light from heaven shone around Saul of Tarsus '... he fell to the ground' (Acts 9:4). Then he heard the voice saying, '... rise and stand on your feet' (Acts 26:16). That is how every life of witness for the Lord begins. It means first falling down on our face before the Lord Jesus at conversion, then standing up on our feet on His behalf, with a view to lifelong service for Him in the strength and glory of the new nature.

However, it must not simply be as individuals in a life of personal witness, quite independent of others. For the boards were placed alongside one another, so that together they might form the integrated supporting structure. This was foreshadowing a New Testament truth, pinpointed for example in 1 Peter 2:5, '... you also, as living stones, are being built up a spiritual house'.

Gold-covered boards lying around could never in that way have formed the Tabernacle structure. Living stones, children of God partaking of the divine nature but experiencing only a life of personal testimony, have to be built up and built together with others of a like kind if they are to form the spiritual house of God. For that reason in Acts 2:41, 'Then those who gladly received his word were baptized; and that day about three thousand souls were added to them'.

The word 'add' here means 'to place additionally, i.e., lay alongside'. In Jerusalem the baptized disciples, when added to the church of God there, were placed alongside those who had enjoyed the same experience; standing by each other, shoulder to shoulder, nothing between, reflecting as mirrors the glory of the Lord - spiritually gold-covered boards standing up and placed side by side with others.

The strength of the gold-covered boards did not depend alone on the mutual support the one gave to the other. The two tenons of each board were firmly bedded in the weighty silver sockets. This silver was part of the atonement money as described in Exodus 30:11-16 and as distributed in Exodus 38:25-28. When Peter in the first chapter of his first epistle (1 Pet.1:18} contrasts the true redemption as found in Christ with the shadowy redemption of silver and gold, he may well have had

THE PARABLE OF THE TABERNACLE 77

these portions in mind regarding the silver and Numbers 31:50 regarding the gold.

This atonement or redemption money was in respect of '... everyone included in the numbering' (Ex.38:26). These were men from twenty years old and upward who had already been redeemed by the blood of the Passover lambs in Egypt. Now they were being numbered for God's service in various forms and they were called upon to pay the silver half shekel, '... every man shall give a ransom for himself' (Ex.30:12).

This was an aspect of redemption associated with men who were already redeemed, as we shall consider later. Meantime it is worthy of note that in the New Testament, numbering has to do with persons being added to churches of God - see Acts 2:41; 4:4; 5:14. The various aspects of the boards, arising directly and indirectly, do not foreshadow simply believers as members of the Church the Body but rather disciples who have a part in God's spiritual house.

There were 603,550 men involved in this numbering, so the half shekel from each provided a sum of 301,775 shekels. With 3,000 shekels equal to one talent this represented 100 talents and 1775 shekels. The total was distributed this way:

- For the 96 sockets under the 48 boards - 96 talents
- For the sockets under the pillars for the veil - 4 talents
- For the hooks, capitals and fillets of the pillars of the court - 1775 shekels

So the boards did not stand on the shifting desert sand, but each one rested on two weighty talents of silver, the ransom money, the redemption accomplished by the Lord Jesus Christ. Not in this case simply redemption from the penalty of sin, for, as we have seen, the silver stood related to the ransom money for those already redeemed by blood from Egypt. Rather it relates to those aspects of redemption viewed in the

New Testament concerning the believer. In Galatians 1:3,4 Paul writes, '... our Lord Jesus Christ, who gave Himself for our sins, that He might deliver us from this present evil age, according to the will of our God and Father'. Again he writes in Titus 2:14, '... who gave Himself for us, that He might redeem us from every lawless deed and purify for Himself His own special people, zealous for good works'. The disciple stands securely on the Person of the Lord Jesus Christ, in His weighty redeeming, delivering power, by means of which he can live in separation from the world, unspotted by its defilements, maintained in upright integrity of testimony.

A further interesting point arises in connection with the word socket. It derives from a Hebrew word meaning lord, master or owner. Thus, disciples in the house of God are founded also on an appreciation and acknowledgment of the lordship of Christ. He is '... the only Lord God and our Lord Jesus Christ' (Jude 4). It is His teaching that is the sole basis of their life and conduct. '... Jesus Christ is Lord' is how Paul summed up the matter in Philippians 2:11.

Then there were the five gold-covered bars of acacia wood, held in place by the rings of pure gold. In the typical teaching from the bars we suggest that, according to the principles of interpretation which we are following, the basic acacia wood will lead us to the Person of the Lord in His Manhood or to men in the likeness of that Manhood. It must correspond with something in the New Testament that binds the disciples together, visibly and invisibly.

We write with very great respect for the views of some who have seen foreshadowed in the bars such doctrinal features as, for example, the four continual things in Acts 2:42, or the four virtues in Ephesians 4:2. It is difficult to follow how the acacia wood can at this point become typical of doctrinal principles.

THE PARABLE OF THE TABERNACLE

Doubtless because of this some have seen typified in the bars the gifts to the Church as in Ephesians 4:11, apostles, prophets, evangelists, pastors and teachers. Others have considered the derivation of the word bars and have, as a consequence, viewed them as picturing ministering servants of the Lord itinerating round all the churches and supported by them, as seen in the golden rings.

The writer enjoys the view of others that in the bars is foreshadowed the elders of the churches in their rule. First in the charge of those disciples allotted to them in the local church (e.g. Phil. 1:1); then in their wider provincial care (e.g. Acts 11:30); and finally in their churches-wide responsibility for the maintenance of unity of teaching and practice in the house of God (e.g. 1 Pet.1:1; 1 Pet.5:1).

It is noteworthy too that the bars went through the rings of gold that were on each board. By divine arrangement, there should be a close personal link between the disciple and the shepherds who care. The work of elders in their rule, shepherds in their care, was put to Peter by the Lord in John 21:15-17 as feeding and tending, two quite different words. Feeding the flock from the Scriptures must always be a vital part of the work of the elders. But in tending to their needs there is an ever-present wide field of personal help to the individual disciple.

The unseen bar of acacia wood was also binding all the boards together. Many lovely thoughts have been expressed regarding the counterpart today. Some have seen in this the Holy Spirit in His great unseen unifying influence. Others have contemplated spiritual virtues that have the effect of binding the saints together. These thoughts have afforded much pleasure to many and are referred to because of our respect for those who enjoyed them. If, however, the principle of uniform interpretation of the type is to be followed, and we write suggestively then the acacia wood in the hidden bar would call for a foreshadowing of some aspect of the Lord Jesus; to some precious revealed truth such as '... Christ in you' (Col.1:27).

The living Christ is in all the disciples strengthening them, binding them, enabling them to maintain the unity of the Spirit in the bond of peace, while seeking also to attain unto the unity of the faith. There we leave the matter for further meditation by the reader.

As we leave this brief study of the boards and their typical teaching for us today, we revert finally to one point - that is the value of the strengthening corner boards. These were boards exactly like all the rest, but they had a unique place in strengthening the structure for God. Strengthening boards are needed in all the churches of God, forming God's house today. Brethren and sisters who can be depended upon in the support of the work of the assembly in all its aspects, to whom others can turn for help, advice, comfort and guidance, the habit of whose life is not to forsake the assembling of the saints together. Maybe as you read this you will be led in deep exercise to pray, 'Lord, make me a strengthening and standing board in Your house, by Your help and grace'.

Note

(2) For 'furtherance' in Phil 1:5 RV, see also Vine

CHAPTER 18: THE THREE ENTRANCES

The gate of the court: Exodus 27:16; 38:18,19

The screen for the door of the tent: Exodus 26:36; 36:37,38

The veil: Exodus 26:31-35; 36:35,36

The old bloodstained way to God was by means of three entrances, each one leading to areas of increased holiness, with diminishing access at the second and third entrances. They were all made of the same material, the veil having in addition the figures of the cherubim embroidered upon it. They had all the same surface area.

The first was made of blue, and purple, and scarlet, and fine linen thread, the work of the embroiderer. It was supported by four pillars, doubtless of acacia wood, resting on four sockets of bronze. The emphasis in the surface area was its width. It measured twenty cubits wide by five cubits high, the latter being the height of the surrounding hangings of the court. Its lovely embroidered colours stood out attractive in their brightness for all to see. The youngest child of years of understanding, the frailest old man in his deep appreciation, the most ashamed and hesitant sinner in his contrition could with the utmost ease draw aside that screen and go to the priest at the bronze altar. The altar was for all, so the entrance was wide and inviting.

The godly Israelite loved to come through that entrance for he felt he was coming close to God. It led to the altar and the courts of the Lord's house where he could bring his burnt offerings, and pay his vows in freewill offerings. From the priest he could receive back the portion of his peace offering on which he and his wife and family could eat, in fellowship with the priests, and in a deeper sense in fellowship with his

God. There also he could bring his sin offerings when he became conscious of trespass in any of the commandments of the Lord. Activity at the altar had a spiritual significance in Israel.

Ahead of the worshipper lay the high entrance to the Holy Place of the Tabernacle and he knew that through that entrance he would never pass. Entrance to the sanctuary was restricted to the priestly sons of Aaron. This second screen, made of exactly the same material as the first, was ten cubits wide by ten cubits high; narrower and higher than the first entrance. It was supported by five pillars of acacia wood overlaid with gold, with golden hooks for the screen, and resting on five sockets of bronze.

As the priest entered the Holy Place, the veil lay ahead of him. Before the veil was the altar of incense. On the north side, to the priest's right hand, was the table of showbread. On the south side stood the golden lampstand. At these units of divine service the priests served twice daily in the case of the altar and the lampstand, and every Sabbath at the table.

The third screen was the veil. Through this, only the high priest of Israel could pass as once a year he entered the Most Holy Place. The purpose of the veil was to divide between the two places and there is a deep significance in that it 'hung' from the clasps. The word veil derives from a Hebrew word meaning 'to break apart; fracture, i.e., severity'. It was the symbol of the broken relationship between God and men by reason of sin. The severe reminder of that deadly fracture faced the priests daily.

The veil was exactly the same size and shape as the second screen. It was made of the same material but it had the embroidered cherubim, those symbolic guardians of the law and the holiness of God. Its golden hooks linked into the golden clasps which bound together the two sets of five coupled Tabernacle curtains and it draped down supported by four pillars of acacia wood overlaid with gold and resting on four sockets of silver. Its position in relation to the golden clasps determined the length of the Most Holy Place, and that it formed a cube ten cubits long, wide and high. Solomon's 'inner sanctuary' was comparable in principle though contrasted in measurement being twenty cubits long, wide and high (1 Kgs 6:20); and the coming city of Revelation 21:16, 'And he measured the city with the reed: twelve thousand furlongs. Its length, breadth, and height are equal'.

The great day of entry within the veil was known as the Day of Atonement, being the tenth day of the seventh month. The ritual is described in remarkably specific detail in Leviticus 16 and will repay close study by the reader. Aaron the high priest bathed first at the laver, then put on the linen garments. Some years ago an issue of a magazine published by 'Friends of Israel' showed the high priest in the Most Holy Place with his garments of glory. One of their readers wrote, "Get the high priest out of the Holy of Holies. He'll die in there!" The reader of course was right and an apology appeared.

It would be impossible to describe the emotional experience of the high priest on the morning of that tenth day. One slip in procedure could mean death. First he presented to the Lord his own young bull by which atonement was to be made for himself and his family. Then he took from the congregation the national offering, two he-goats for a sin offering and one ram for a burnt offering. The two goats he set before the Lord at the door of the tent of meeting, then he cast lots to decide which was to be for the Lord and go to the altar and which was to be for 'dismissal' (Lev.16:8 RV margin; 'the scapegoat' NKJV) into the solitary land.

This complete, the high priest killed the young bull that was his own sin offering. Then he took a censer full of live coals from the bronze altar and, filling his hands full of sweet incense beaten small, he drew aside the veil and laid the censer with its incense before the Lord. Thus, he created a new veil within, a veil of incense in the divine presence. He could only minister in the Most Holy Place in the cloud of that incense, otherwise he would die. Then he came out and collected the blood of the sacrificed young hull and returned to sprinkle it with his finger on the east side of the mercy seat and seven times on the ground before it. Then he came out again and this time slew the goat of the people's sin offering which was for the Lord and returned to the Most Holy Place and sprinkled the goat's blood as he had sprinkled the young bull's.

No one else was allowed in the Most Holy Place with him. Cedar wood and hyssop were not to be used to sprinkle the blood, simply the finger of the priest. Nothing extraneous was allowed save only the presence of the high priest and the essential blood and incense. And 'as far as the east is from the west' (Ps.103:12) so far did God remove by His ritual the transgressions of His people as they affected His Most Holy Place. Then the high priest went out into the Holy Place and made atonement also for '... the altar that is before the LORD' (Lev.16:18), i.e., the altar of incense, as distinct from '... the altar that is by the door of the tabernacle of meeting' (Lev. 1:5), i.e., the bronze altar. He put the blood of young bull and goat on the horns of the altar, then seven times he sprinkled the blood with his finger on the altar itself and in this way atonement was made for the Holy Place.

Then he took the goat for dismissal and, laying both his hands heavily on its head, he confessed over it all the iniquities, transgressions and sins of the nation of Israel. A man who was standing by in readiness took the scapegoat, as it is usually called, bearing on itself all the wrongs of Israel, and led it away to a solitary land where he left it alone to die. As Israel watched the one goat go, carrying away their sins in the forbearance of God, they could see publicly in relation to their own defilement, what God had done in the secrecy of the sanctuary in relation to its defilements, with the blood of the other goat. Then the veil closed for another year.

THE PARABLE OF THE TABERNACLE 85

For the 500 years of the Tabernacle service, the veil hung under the golden clasps. Then another veil was made for Solomon's Temple: '... of blue, purple, crimson, and fine linen, and wove cherubim into it' (2 Chr.3:14). In addition, two doors of olive wood were provided for '... the entrance of the inner sanctuary' (1 Kgs. 6:31), with various ornate carvings and all covered with gold. So long as the veil hung, the way of the holies into the presence of God was not visible for all to see, far less available for all to tread. The veil had to remain for all those long centuries of animal sacrifice when sin was being passed over in the forbearance of God (Rom.3:25), until the question of sin could be finally dealt with by virtue of the great atonement of the Lord Jesus Christ at Calvary as the basis upon which remission of sins would become available for all who would trust Him.

> 'Now it was about the sixth hour, and there was darkness over all the earth until the ninth hour. Then the sun was darkened, and the veil of the temple was torn in two. And when Jesus had cried out with a loud voice, He said, "Father, 'into Your hands I commit My spirit.'" Having said this, He breathed His last' (Lk.23:44-46).

So Tabernacle and Temple days were over. The days of the old slain way through the limited access of the three entrances were over. The words that but a few days before Jesus had spoken to unrepentant Israel became final: 'See! Your house is left to you desolate ...' (Lk.13:35). The old covenant too was now '... ready to vanish away' (Heb. 8:13).

We have considered the third screen in somewhat greater detail for it is one of the most sacred of all the Tabernacle types. We should now look at the teaching foreshadowed in the case of each of the three screens. In all three we see God reaching out to man from His dwelling place in the sanctuary inviting him to come near to Him on prescribed conditions and within prescribed limitations. In that sense, beginning from the sanctuary we see the Lord Jesus Christ as '... the way, the truth, and the life. No one comes to the Father except through Me' (John 14:6).

On the other hand, from the human standpoint, the Lord Jesus is always ahead of men, beckoning them forward, willing to lead them on and in to the aspect of the service of God which is appropriate to them. At the first entrance men take their first step to God, to the Christ at the bronze altar, to the great Sin-bearer; in Him they find their Substitute and by His stripes they are healed (all of Isaiah 53 is appropriate here). All this is presented to them by the four intimate, factual accounts of the Saviour's life story as told by the four gospel narrators.

There is something to be said for those who have seen these four men prefigured in the four supporting pillars of acacia wood, holding up for all to see the glories of the first entrance.

It has pleased the Lord to give to every born-again person the full potential rights to serve as a priest in His holy priesthood. In both Tabernacle and Temple the house of God was for the priesthood. That was the place of their collective service. They served in divisions (1 Chr.24:7-19) but every individual priest had an active place in the collective priesthood. The New Testament counterpart of this, we suggest, is found for example, in 1 Peter 2:5, '... you also, as living stones, are being built up a spiritual house, a holy priesthood, to offer up spiritual sacrifices acceptable to God through Jesus Christ'. So the new convert is invited to follow the pattern of New Testament teaching, in the strict sequence of the well-known and much-loved steps of Acts 2:41,42:

- 'Then those who gladly
- received his word
- were baptized;
- and that day about three thousand souls
- were added to them.
- And they continued steadfastly

THE PARABLE OF THE TABERNACLE 87

- in the apostles' doctrine
- and (Greek - the) fellowship,
- (Greek - and) in the breaking of bread,
- and in (Greek - the) prayers.'

On being 'added' they were 'joined' to the Church of God in Jerusalem. A few years later the former persecutor in the same city '... tried to join the disciples' (Acts 9:26). The word join means 'to glue or cement together' and is used of the marriage bond. It would not have admitted any thought of occasional fellowship or a limited fellowship in the Church in Jerusalem and, at the same time, were this possible, an alliance with others elsewhere. It meant a dedication to the Church in Jerusalem and to churches of God in every place, in a loyalty of separation to their understanding of the whole counsel of God.

These disciples in the Church of God in Jerusalem found themselves in due course in a growing fellowship of assemblies, all of them described by Paul as 'God's building' (1 Cor. 3:9), and in Christ Jesus '... in whom the whole ('each' RV) building, being fitted together, grows into a holy temple in the Lord' (Eph.2:21). This then was the spiritual house (as distinct from the Church the Body) in which the individual believer could function as a priest in the holy and the royal priesthood.

Thus, in the language of the type, he could go through the second screen and engage in the priestly service. This screen was high, in contrast to the first screen, which was wide. It represented Christ still ahead, leading on to the place of His lordship, Christ the Truth. It is a sad commentary on the affections of many of God's dear children that His truth after conversion is neither popular nor palatable in all its parts. Many have become selective in their choice as to which aspects of the whole counsel of God they should accept and pursue. Were it not for such scriptures as 2 Timothy 4:3 it would be difficult to conceive why professing believers have turned off completely at step two, that is, baptism by immersion.

How can anyone expect to be in the spiritual house of God today, for the functioning of the holy priesthood, if they decline to take their place through baptism by immersion in a local church of God, built according to the pattern of teaching which operated by the authority of the risen Lord from the Church of God in Jerusalem onwards, outwards?

We write with even greater tenderness when we think of many near and dear to us, from whose spiritual forefathers our own forefathers separated in 1892-94. These beloved brethren are sound on conversion, in the main on baptism before reception, zealous exceedingly in maintaining the work of the local autonomous assembly, but acknowledging nothing of a corporate nature in the New Testament beyond that, save the Church the Body.

From the various scriptures to which attention has been earlier drawn, it is evident that in the New Testament the local churches of God formed collectively, albeit conditionally as Hebrews 3:6 indicates, the house of God, and the disciples in the churches collectively formed the holy priesthood. This is part of the faith once for all delivered to the saints (Jude 3) and should therefore remain the pattern of collective witness for God till the close of the present dispensation. The churches of God, the house of God, the holy priesthood comprise the same people. Over them is the Lord Jesus Christ as Son over God's house (Heb.3:6 RV margin] and as Great Priest over the house of God (Heb.10:21 RV margin). The holy priesthood renders all its service to God through Him. He has entered within the veil as a forerunner for us (Heb.6:20). He is '... seated at the right hand of the throne of the Majesty in the heavens, a Minister of the sanctuary and of the true tabernacle which the Lord erected, and not man' (Heb.8:1,2).

As High Priest of the good things to come He has entered once for all into the holies (Heb.9:11,12). He has '... not entered the holy places made with hands, which are copies of the true, but into heaven itself, now to appear in the presence of God for us' (Heb.9:24). The holy priesthood in New Testament days gathered locally as priests in the churches of God to which they individually belonged. When they assembled themselves together, as Hebrews 10:25 puts it, they were said to be '... together as a church' (1 Cor.11:18).

On such occasions they carried out their priestly responsibilities and God saw them in their priesthood unity. They gathered on earth in their assemblies but the place of their service was in the heavenly sanctuary; in the 'true tabernacle', which the Lord erected, not man. So it was not a question of Jesus in their midst in the local assembly; rather they were drawing near in spirit to where He was in the presence of God.

This is beautifully set out in Hebrews 10:19-22. Those addressed are the people of God forming the house of God on earth. On the glorious basis of the remission of sins we read, 'Therefore, brethren, having boldness to enter the Holiest by the blood of Jesus, by a new and living way which He consecrated for us, through the veil, that is, His flesh, and having a High Priest over the house of God, let us draw near ...'

In contrast to the old bloodstained way from the gate of the court stopping short at the veil, there is now the way of the holies made available for the holy priesthood, leading right in to the immediate presence of God. The basis of access is the blood of Jesus. There is still a veil, but that veil is the flesh of Christ. He is before God on behalf of His people, a Great Priest over the holy priesthood.

As the people of God gather on the first day of the week to break bread, we have the glorious opportunity of drawing near with a Spirit-begotten boldness and joy, to present to our Great Priest our worship and spiritual sacrifices, which He offers for us to the God and Father of our Lord Jesus Christ. There on the table lie the symbols of our approach: the bread - His flesh; the wine - His blood.

We note then the difference from Tabernacle days. Then the priesthood of Aaron came into God's house at stated times for specific purposes; some into the first section, and the high priest only through the veil into the second, one day in the year. Today the holy priesthood actually forms God's house, and though its members gather in their local assemblies for service God-ward, that service is conducted '...in spirit and truth' (John 4:24).

in the heavenly sanctuary above. Not a sanctuary divided by a separating veil, but one sanctuary known as the Holy Place (Greek - the holies] where Jesus the Son of God is the Veil through whom we draw near to worship. As H. Bonar so well expressed it:

> "The gate is open wide,
>
> The new and living way
>
> Is clear and free and bright
>
> With love and peace and day.
>
> Into the Holies now we come -
>
> Our present and eternal home."
>
> (H. Bonar, PHSS 61)

CHAPTER 19: THE LAMPSTAND OF PURE GOLD

Exodus 25:31-40; 27:20,21; 37:17-24; 40:24,25; Leviticus 24:1-4

The Holy Place was lit by the light from the seven-branched lampstand. This was a preparation of exquisite beauty and marvellous craftsmanship. Moses saw its shape and size in the pattern on the mount. He received commandment that there must be no departure from this and it was to be made, including its accessories, from a talent of pure gold. Only three of the major articles in the Tabernacle were made entirely of pure gold, as distinct from being overlaid with gold. They were the lampstand, the mercy seat and the covering cherubim. The mercy seat appears to have been simply a slab of pure gold. But the other two were intricate '... hammered work' (Ex.25:18,31).

The word means 'moulded by hammering'. A brilliant unnamed craftsman patiently and gently hammered out, beat by beat, the block of pure gold into every single intricacy of the ornate design of the pure lampstand. The British Parliament gifted the Knesset of the newly formed State of Israel a Menorah (Lampstand) in 1956 but it was not of beaten work of pure gold! It required a Spirit-filled Aholiab to instruct the beating out of the Tabernacle lampstand.

It had a centre shaft and base and on the shaft were four cups that resembled almond-blossom. With each cup was a knob and a flower. The word knob comes from a Hebrew word meaning 'to encircle', so it was probably disc-shaped. Six branches went out from the central shaft, one on each side at each of the three lower knobs. (Some will be interested to note that the word translated 'going out' in Exodus 25:32 RV is, in the Septuagint, the same Greek word as 'proceeds from' in John 15:26).

Each of the six branches had three cups, knobs and flowers. Seven lamps were placed, one on the top of the central shaft and one on the top of each of the six branches. There is no indication as to whether the seven lamps lay in a straight line. It has been inferred, however, that this was the case, since the representation of the lampstand in the figures on the triumphal Arch of Titus in Rome, erected after the destruction of Jerusalem, showed the lamps in uniform height. One thing is clear, the light from the seven lamps burned together as one. There were also wick-trimmers and trays. Everything was meticulously made out of the talent of pure gold. There has always been diversity of view as to the modern equivalent of the ancient Hebrew weights. The IVP New Bible Dictionary gives 30kg as the equivalent of one talent,[8] and this is probably sufficiently accurate for our purpose.

It was the responsibility of the people to ensure that a constant supply of pure olive oil was beaten out and brought to the priests, so that the lamps on the lampstand might burn continually. Without the vital oil the lampstand in all its beauty would have been totally ineffective. This supply was one of the 'continual' or 'perpetual' things specifically referred to as such and enjoined on Israel to maintain.

We refer to:

- The continual showbread - Ex.25:30; 2 Chr.2:4.
- The lamp to burn continually - Ex.27:20.
- The breastplate ... before the LORD continually - Ex.28:29.
- Two lambs ... day by day continually - Ex.29:38.
- A perpetual incense - Ex.30:8.
- Fire ... on the altar; it shall never go out - Lev.6:13

The unbroken continuity of these services was vital, for in them God rested, feasting continually on the glories and perfections of the great substance of the True who was coming one day to make all things new.

THE PARABLE OF THE TABERNACLE 93

According to Exodus 30:7-8 it was the responsibility of the high priest to dress the lamps every morning and to light them every evening. From this some have concluded that the lamps only burned from evening until morning, and it was priestly responsibility to keep the light alive all the hours of darkness. This assumes that some of the bright daylight of the East filtered through the screen at the door of the tent. Others have thought that the emphasis laid on the continual aspect of the burning lamps, the need for steady light for the service of the Holy Place not dependent on conditions outside, points rather to lamps which burned day and night, the priest trimming the burning wick in the morning and lighting with fresh oil in the evening. The basic fact remains that the purpose of the lampstand was to '... give light in front of it' (Ex.25:37); that is at the table of showbread, the altar of incense and at the veil, and in its light the service of God was carried out.

The lamps were to burn continually, day after day, century after century. But that was the ideal and many a time the disinterested nation ceased to bring the oil and the indifferent priests let the sanctuary lights go out. The spluttering lights in the night when God called Samuel were only symptomatic of the condition of priests and people. A neglected sanctuary service needed no burning lights. Solomon's beautiful Temple had only been in service some thirty years when ten of the twelve tribes hived off and set up an idolatrous substitute priestly service. They had no concern for the true lampstand and its oil and the service of God on which it shone.

We leave the narrative side on a brighter note by reference to Zechariah's well-known fifth vision (Zech.4). It featured a lampstand all of gold but rather different from the one in the Tabernacle. It had a bowl on the top that ensured a fuller and more steady supply of oil. It was a sort of reservoir into which oil flowed from two olive trees alongside, representing Joshua and Zerubbabel. Pipes then led the oil from it to each of the seven lamps. When Zechariah enquired the meaning of the vision the angel answered, 'This is the word of the LORD to Zerubbabel: "Not by might nor by power, but by My Spirit," says the LORD of hosts' (Zech. 4:6). This portion is not only a stimulation to the spirit in every age, but a valuable piece of internal interpretation also.

Is there anything in the true Tabernacle in heavenly places to which the Tabernacle lampstand bore similarity? John saw a throne set in heaven and One sitting upon it. Before the throne he saw seven lamps of fire burning '... which are the seven Spirits of God' (Rev.4:5). There is, of course, only one Spirit of God though His unity may be seen in perfect diversity, as, for example, in the seven aspects of Ephesians 4:4-6, and here in the seven lamps of fire. This was the Spirit of God in the sevenfold perfection of uncreated light - the great heavenly Lampstand.

John also saw in the midst of the throne '... stood a Lamb as though it had been slain, having seven horns and seven eyes, which are the seven Spirits of God sent out into all the earth' (Rev.5:6). In the seven horns of the Lamb can be seen the perfection of His power and authority. He had also seven eyes which were the seven Spirits of God, again unity in perfect diversity, sent forth by the Lamb into all the earth in the perfection of illumination (compare Matt.6:22). So the heavenly scene presents the great Light Holder in the divine presence, sent forth by the Son to enlighten the minds of earth-dwellers.

In looking into the shadows of the Tabernacle lampstand we must first remember that it was made of pure gold, without any acacia wood, and that its one purpose was to give light for the maintenance of the service of God. It therefore speaks to us of One who is divine and whose great work is to illuminate the minds of disciples in relation to the Person of the Son of God and to the sanctuary service of God. It was the Holy Spirit who was sent forth by the Lord Jesus Christ in His ascension. He explained the position beforehand to His disciples, '... but if I depart,

THE PARABLE OF THE TABERNACLE 95

I will send Him to you. And when He has come, He will convict the world of sin, and of righteousness, and of judgment... He will guide you into all truth... He will glorify Me' (John 16:7,8,13,14).

It was the Holy Spirit who revealed to men the glories of the Son of God, in His Deity in His Manhood; all His spiritual excellencies and moral winsomeness; till the hearts of men began to grow warm in relation to Him. It was the Holy Spirit who illuminated the minds of men regarding conversion and a place in the Church the Body; discipleship and a place in the spiritual house of God. It was He who shed light on the spiritual truths associated with the table and the altar of incense, who showed the significance of the communion in the breaking of the bread and the prayers.

To assist the Spirit in His great work there came forward men and women whom He had Himself enlightened, and they let the Spirit of God flow through them as oil through an unobstructed channel. 'So Jesus said to them again, "Peace to you! As the Father has sent Me, I also send you." And when He had said this, He breathed on them, and said to them, "Receive the Holy Spirit" (John 20:21,22). These were the persons who corresponded to the Israelites in the days of the type who brought the beaten olive oil so that the lamps might never cease to burn, nor the service of God to cease. They corresponded also to Joshua and Zerubbabel, gloriously described as men who emptied the golden oil out of themselves.

Basic to our interpretation of the type we can see the Son of God in the great central shaft, associated with the sending forth of the Holy Spirit, as seen in the seven lamps of burning oil, to enlighten men and women regarding the glories of Christ and the sanctuary service of God and to make them fruitful in their understanding of the whole counsel of God (as foreshadowed in the almond blossom and the flowers).

The Spirit of God Himself supplies a further teaching for us to consider in relation to the lampstand. The seven churches of God in Asia were seen by John in his vision as seven golden lampstands (Rev.1:9-20). Each church was a lampstand, doubtless having seven lamps burning. Each church of God is all of gold in the sense that it is a divine acquisition by means of the blood of the Lord Jesus Christ (Acts 20:28). It can certainly be viewed as hammered work, as one considers the long period of patient work before a church of God can be brought into existence; Paul's eighteen months in Corinth, and his three years in Ephesus.

It is a stand on which lamps are to burn, lights shining with wicks well-trimmed. We saw already the truth of the individual board standing up in fellowship with others to form a church of God in fellowship with other churches of God. So with the lamps, the place for the lamp, the new life burning for Christ, is on the lampstand. The Lord would have His children take their place in one of the churches of God that form His house, and shine in testimony together with others so that a clear combined light might light up the service of God for others to see. It is all in agreement with what we have already considered from 1 Peter 2:5, '... you also, as living stones, are being built up a spiritual house, a holy priesthood'.

The whole point of the lampstand was to give light over against it in the sanctuary so that priestly service could be maintained there. In the New Testament it was the Spirit-given light shining out from churches of God, which illuminated the minds of children of God as to the possibility and nature of priestly service carried out in the heavenly sanctuary by those on earth in God's house. The clear teaching today of the churches of God on, for example, the holy priesthood service has been the means in God's hand of enlightening the minds of many beloved disciples as to the true nature of collective worship in the heavenly sanctuary, as the assembly draws near there on a Lord's day morning at the time of the breaking of the bread.

Alas that so many dear children of God see no further than presenting themselves for one or two sermons delivered for their personal help on the first day of the week. Others picture the Lord in the midst of their assembly when they gather to keep the Remembrance, in an application of Matthew 18:20, out of context.

Golden lampstands beam out the truths running through the epistle to the Hebrews, in accordance with which the people of God are seen as drawing near as a holy priesthood by the new and living way of Hebrews 10:19-22 into the heavenly sanctuary, there to remain for a period of service Godward in the Spirit, offering spiritual sacrifices acceptable to God through Jesus Christ, through Jesus the Son of God who is the Great Priest over the house of God. When the period of drawing near is over and the people of God retire from the heavenly sanctuary, then and not until then is there opportunity to minister the Word among themselves.

In all divine service it is still true that it is: '"... Not by might nor by power, but by My Spirit," says the LORD of hosts' (Zech.4:6). God is still looking for, and graciously depending on, willing disciples who will give priority to nothing in their life that will impede the flow of the Holy Spirit through them. Such disciples store their mind with Christ until He lives in them; they study His Word with patience until His thoughts flow through them. There is a clear call that we keep our lamps clean and ready, wicks trimmed, oil flowing freely, and flames burning clearly and steadily - and in fellowship with the other lamps on the stand, that is, in our own assembly.

In the Revelation aspect of the lampstand it is not simply now shining on the service in the sanctuary of God, but the church of God is right out in the open for all to see. Hence the need for the fruitfulness of the

Spirit in the disciple's life, as envisaged in the almond blossom, and the need for reflecting in an unpleasant world the beauties of our attractive Master, as envisaged in the flowers.

Every church of God has a place in the fellowship of assemblies forming the house of God. That place may be lost. But if a church of God fails in all these things, and in the purity of their affections in relation to them, the warning comes clearly from Revelation 2:5 'I will come ... and remove your lampstand from its place'. Outwardly services may continue apparently as before but the Walker in the midst of His lampstands has noted the gradual declension and the point comes when He moves that lampstand out of its place among the rest. The Church of God in Smyrna referred to in Revelation 2:8-11 continued in its outward form of service and grew into a mighty Bishopric. One of its most notable Bishops was the martyred Polycarp. But the simple pattern of church administration laid down by the Lord had long since been departed from, and no quality of Christian living can replace broken standards.

Since the writing of Hebrews 3:6 disciples should know that churches of God are conditional for their divine recognition on their holding fast to the faith once for all delivered to the saints.

CHAPTER 20: THE TABLE OF SHOWBREAD

Exodus 25:23-30; 37:10-16; Leviticus 24:5-9, 1 Chronicles 9:31,32

The light from the lampstand shone across the Holy Place and its radiance fell on a stately little ornate table. It is the first recorded table in Scripture. It was the Lord's table. It was small, for everything in the Tabernacle was relatively small. It had to be so. Solomon said to God of the vast, magnificent temple he had built, 'Behold, heaven and the heaven of heavens cannot contain You. How much less this temple which I have built!' (1 Kgs 8:27). How very much less was this little Tabernacle structure! Truly the One who was glorious in holiness had also proved Himself to be glorious in lowliness.

The table itself was two cubits long by one cubit broad by one and a half cubits high. It was made of acacia wood, and then covered with pure gold. Experts have pointed out that an ounce of gold may be pounded out in a film so thin that it can cover one hundred square feet. The ancient Egyptians are on record as having hammered gold into leaves so thin that 367,000 made a pile one inch high.

The table surface was protected all round the rim by a moulding, (referred to as a crown in the RV). Then there was a border, a space of a handbreadth in width, then another moulding, or crown, all round. There was thus, a protected part of the table where the showbread was safely supported, and a border all around for holding various utensils. These were the dishes for carrying the bread, the pans for the incense, the pitchers and bowls for the meal offerings and their accompanying drink offerings (Ex.25: 29).

The table stood on four legs and at the top of each leg, close by the border, was a ring of gold, through which the staves were placed when the table was in transit. The attendant dishes, pans and pitchers were all made of pure gold. Certain Kohathites were responsible to ensure that the showbread was baked and ready for placing hot on the table on the Sabbath day (1 Sam.21:6). It consisted of twelve cakes of fine flour. From the derivation of the Hebrew word these would be pierced cakes. Each cake was made from two tenth parts of an ephah of flour, that is, two omers. This was a substantial quantity, for an omer is estimated to be approximately equal to 2 litres. So on the day before the Sabbath the Israelites were gathering two omers of manna for each person, to suffice also for the Sabbath day; the Kohathites were preparing the fine flour for twelve cakes each of two omers as the nation's Sabbath meal offering to their God.

The twelve cakes were placed on the table in two rows, rather than piles, six cakes in each row. The Hebrew word for row simply means 'an arrangement'. Everything related to God and His house in every age is perfect in its orderliness (a point emphasised by Paul in 1 Corinthians 14:33). This arrangement for the cakes was just as much by specific divine requirement as was the disposal of the twelve stones on the breastplate of the high priest. There was arrangement on the table, and a moulding, or crowns for its protection.

The purpose of the showbread would indicate that each of the twelve cakes would be seen separately. The word showbread comes from two Hebrew words, food and the face. It has become generally known then as the bread of faces, the presence-bread, and in agreement with this God instructed that the twelve cakes were to be set upon the table '... before Me (Heb. My face) always' (Ex. 25:30).

Pure frankincense was placed on the top of each cake as it was laid on the table. From various records it can be taken that the frankincense was white (as the derivation of the word shows}; that it was a vegetable resin of bitter taste but termed frank because of the freeness with which

THE PARABLE OF THE TABERNACLE 101

it gave off its perfume when burned; it was also used in olden times to dispel unpleasant odours. After the seven days it may have been removed from the top of the showbread just as icing is lifted from a cake. It was then placed on the altar of incense, '...an offering made by fire to the LORD' (Lev. 24:7).

So instead of the twelve cakes going to the altar, the frankincense alone was taken and thus became '... on the bread for a memorial, an offering made by fire to the LORD' (op. cit.). The memorial was the portion selected from the offering to go to the altar of God. It comes from a Hebrew root, to mark, i.e., to remember, so that the memorial was a remembrance offering. Every Sabbath day, God feasted at the bronze altar morning and evening on the Lamb who was coming one day (already '... slain from the foundation of the world' (Rev.13:8)) and whose death would be the basis of the great atonement. So in His forbearance He passed over the sins of the people as their sacrifices came to the altar. Meantime in the sanctuary at the pure table He was feasting on the great Meal Offering who was coming; on that fragrant Life, crushed, bruised, ground, sifted, all in unbroken fellowship with the Father's will. So He bore with the murmurings of a disobedient people. In their life in the camp, Israel should have corresponded to the purity of the fine flour that they had sent into the sanctuary in the twelve cakes. But they did not. All down the disastrous years they had to be '... accepted in the Beloved' (Eph. 1:6) who was coming. Meantime while God feasted in this way, the priests also feasted on the old cakes, still fresh, in a holy place. Not the Holy Place; for wherever a priest lived was to be a holy place. It was a time of communion in relation to the table.

It pleased God to regard this whole ceremony in a unique way, as '... being taken from the children of Israel by an everlasting covenant' (Lev. 24:8). His covenant with Israel was bilateral; it was conditional. Inside the ark of the covenant were the two tables of the testimony containing the ten commandments. They were safe there, and unbroken. God would never take the initiative in departing from His responsibilities in terms of the covenant of Sinai. Outside in the camp Israel broke these commandments every day, continually unfaithful to their covenant commitment.

But God looked down on the twelve pierced cakes in the Holy Place, Israel's national offering, and was prepared to view with equal favour each of the twelve tribes as in an acceptable condition of covenant relationship with Himself. So He put up with their ways' (Acts 13:18), and a failing people were permitted to enjoy what Isaiah later wrote, 'In the LORD all the descendants of Israel shall be justified, and shall glory' (Isa.45:25). The assessment of Balaam held good, 'He has not observed iniquity in Jacob, nor has He seen wickedness in Israel' (Num.23:21).

In the shadows of this typical portion our hearts are immediately lifted up in gratitude to God as we think of the glorious Person of the Lord Jesus Christ who came to earth to fulfil the type and is now supporting His people in their service in the heavenly sanctuary. It is remarkable how, in representing them before the face of God, He is named in Hebrews 4:14-16 as Jesus the Son of God. This is truly the table of acacia wood overlaid with pure gold, and bearing the double crown. Here is the resurrected Man of Calvary, restored to His place in glory alongside the Father, crowned with glory and honour. A Man in the Glory! This same Jesus! We marvel when we look up to the moon and think that human feet have trod it, if even a little. But what of the Man whom the King delights to honour? (see Est.6:6). We ponder the dual mystery; God in human form among men; and a Man in human form, albeit glorified, on the throne of God. There He is, supporting His people, as the table did the bread, as their Advocate and Great High Priest. It is by reason of His life that we are preserved in the service of God (Rom.5:10).

THE PARABLE OF THE TABERNACLE

Not only did the table uphold before the face of God the twelve tribes, which were symbolised in the twelve cakes, but the cakes were to God for a meal offering, which foreshadowed to Him His Son in the gentle days of His flesh. This meal offering became later the portion of the priests. Correspondingly, it is the great privilege of disciples today to share with God His appreciation of His beloved Son. To read of the perfections of the life of the Man Jesus, to meditate on His excellencies to the point of personal assimilation, and to feast on His character and ways till these begin to be reflected in us. We can show to the world some strong evidence of what God sees us to be in Christ. That is why Paul speaks of Christ formed in him; living in him; revealed in him; magnified in him; '... that the life of Jesus also may be manifested in our body' (2 Cor. 4:10).

> There's a Man in the Glory
>
> Whose life is for me.
>
> He's pure and He's holy,
>
> Triumphant and free.
>
> He's wise and He's loving,
>
> Tender is He;
>
> And His life in the Glory
>
> My life may be.
>
> There's a Man in the Glory
>
> Whose life is for me.
>
> His peace is abiding,
>
> Patient is He.

He's joyful and radiant,

Expecting to see

His life in the Glory

Lived out in me.

(Attributed to various authors)

There is a further principle, rather than a foreshadowing, which arises in considering the 'pure gold table before the LORD' as in Leviticus 24:6; '... My table ...' as in Ezekiel 44:16. It is that in God's house in Israel's day there was a service in relation to the Lord's table and a similar expression and a form of service is found in connection with the New Testament house. Paul says, '... you cannot partake of the Lord's table and of the table of demons' (1 Cor.10:21). The thought behind the word table is that of communion in eating. In the Tabernacle we have already noted that there was an orderly arrangement in connection with the table. This applies equally in the spiritual house.

Today the Lord has set His table within His house where it stands related to the breaking of the bread. There was a protective arrangement on the Tabernacle table for the bread. It is evident also that there is an arrangement for the breaking of the bread as an ordinance of divine service in the New Testament churches of God. It was the privilege of those who had been saved, baptized by immersion and added to the local church of God.

It has been expressed well that at the institution of the ordinance in the Upper Room we see the precious gem itself. In the breaking of the bread in the Church of God in Jerusalem in Acts 2:42 we see the gem in the beauty of its proper setting. It is not a question of men legislating who should break bread together. It is a specific New Testament arrangement that the Lord has laid down in the pattern and it is His wish that it be adhered to. Nowhere is there any reference to the Father's table in the New Testament, as though the determining factor is whether or not the worshipper is a child of God. Far less is there any Scripture that suggests that a person is free to take communion provided he or she was sprinkled as an infant, is now a resultant member of the particular church, yet may not be saved at all.

We invite the reader's attention to the fact that it is disciples baptized by immersion and added to a church of God, and thus part of God's spiritual house, who are legislated for in Scripture as breaking bread according to the divine mind, as in Acts 2:42; 20:7; 1 Corinthians 11:23-33. Naturally, most believers have a strong desire to remember the Lord in the breaking of the bread. And that is good and as it ought to be. But we must be faithful to one another in our clear understanding as to where God has arranged that the ordinance should be kept. It is one aspect of divine service that is part of the arrangements of God's spiritual house.

What a moment it was when the priest took the golden spoon and, removing the pure frankincense from the old bread, presented it to God as a sweet fragrance on the altar of incense. And what a moment it is on a Lord's day morning when after a brief spell of reverent quiet as we prepare to draw near into the holies, a brother goes to the table on behalf of the assembly, gives thanks for the bread, breaks it and it passes from hand to hand in a sweet communion of the body of Christ!

Then he returns to the table and gives thanks for the wine, pours the cup and, as the vessels pass from hand to hand, we have a precious communion in the blood of Christ. It is like taking the frankincense from the pierced cakes and laying it on the fire from the bronze altar so that the fragrance of Christ may arise. Brethren and sisters, part of the holy priesthood, have as it were their golden spoon to offer some frankincense to the God and Father of our Lord Jesus Christ; some fresh, warm appreciation of the excellencies of our Beloved, some things they have made '... concerning the King' (Ps.45:1).

The whole company is in a meditative silence, save as exercised brethren lead the assembly in a freshness of worship which corresponds to the fresh cakes on the Sabbath day or some hymns of fragrant remembrance. Then we go home and feast on the Christ who sustains us.

O God, what perfect rest is Thine!

Thy rest is in Thy Son;

'Tis all unspeakable, divine,

Thy rest and ours are one.

Inside the circle of Thy love

Joined to His life are we above;

How sweet with Thee, O God, to share

Thy joy which is Thy portion there!

Thou findest in that spotless One,

Where all perfections dwell,

All that Thy heart could wish for us,

All that Thou e'er couldst tell;

Thou findest ransomed, righteous, fair,

Where all Thy joys transcendent are,

In Him a people for Thy praise,

Thy glory through eternal days.

(J. Denham Smith, PHSS 76)

CHAPTER 21: THE ALTAR OF INCENSE

The light from the lampstand fell also on the relatively tall, graciously figured altar of incense. It measured only one cubit in breadth and length but two cubits in height. It was made of acacia wood, overlaid with pure gold. Round its top surface was a moulding described as a crown in the RV, and there was a horn at each corner made of one piece with the altar. There were staves of acacia wood overlaid with gold, and these went through two rings of gold on each of two sides for carrying the altar when it was in transit.

The altar was placed '... before the veil that is before the ark of the Testimony, before the mercy seat that is over the Testimony, where I will meet with you' (Ex. 30:6). The location in the Holy Place was precise and instructive. The altar of incense had an immediate association with the mercy seat. Furthermore, the bronze altar and the altar of incense had a connection daily, but the altar of incense had a unique blood connection annually with the mercy seat.

The daily connection was at the time of the morning and evening sacrifice, when the lamb was being sacrificed on the bronze altar, and, as we noted, burned as incense. At the same time a censer was filled with fire from the altar and the incense laid on it. The censer was then placed on the top of the golden altar and its fragrance filled the Holy Place. So although the purpose of the two altars was different they nevertheless had this in common. From them both the fragrant incense went up to God from two quite different sources. The fragrance of the One who was coming deeply satisfied Him.

The annual connection was when the high priest on the Day of Atonement had completed his service in the Most Holy Place, he came out and sprinkled some of the blood of the same bull and goat on the horns of '... the altar that is before the LORD' (Lev.16:18), that is, the altar of incense. Seven times he sprinkled the blood with his finger, cleansing, hallowing, and making atonement for it, because of all the defilements of the children of Israel. Clearly the altar of incense had an intimate relationship with God and His holy dwelling, a point confirmed by the statement in 1 Kings 6:22 that in Solomon's Temple the golden altar belonged to the inner sanctuary, that is, the Most Holy Place.

Within the Holy Place, morning and evening, while the priest attended to the requirements of the lampstand, incense of sweet spices had at the same time to be offered on the altar of incense. It was to be a perpetual incense throughout their generations. Apart from the prescribed incense the only other thing that was to burn on the altar was the frankincense from the showbread weekly.

The prescribed incense was composed of four sweet spices: stacte, onycha, galbanum and frankincense, a like amount of each. It was to be seasoned with salt, then beaten very small, '... incense ... according to the art of the perfumer' (Ex.30:35). A supply was to be kept before the veil and used daily as required. The composition was uniquely for the Lord. Not only were they not to make it for themselves, but they were simply not to make it at all. Should anyone make it and smell it he would be cut off from his people.

It is interesting to note the value the Israelite put on the fragrance of the incense to God. David wrote, 'Let my prayer be set before You as incense, the lifting up of my hands as the evening sacrifice' (Ps.141:2). And as David lifted up his hands in personal prayer, he longed that these prayers might be acceptable to God, after the manner of the incense at the two altars. This association in the psalmist's mind between prayer and incense showed great spiritual insight in the ways of God.

In all probability personal prayer was prevalent among the God-fearing Israelites, but there was no instruction in the law for collective prayer.

Nevertheless in the opening verses of Luke's gospel we see that a very pleasant exercise had arisen in Israel, somewhat of a development of David's personal vision. Zacharias, the old priest, was of Abijah's eighth division in the priestly arrangement. Eight speaks of the new thing; the eighth day was the renewed first day of the week. There were eight persons mentioned as connected with the beginning of the new dispensation; Zacharias, Elisabeth, Joseph, Mary, Simeon, Anna, John and Jesus. While Zacharias was offering the evening incense the whole multitude of the people were praying outside. The nation appeared, like David, to associate prayer with incense, doubtless longing that the acceptance by God of the incense would be extended by Him to their prayers also. Actually this was what Zacharias experienced. For an angel stood at the right side of the altar. The word right derives from 'to receive'. Normally the right hand is given in reception or for acceptance. So it was that his prayer had been accepted and was shortly to be answered.

What is there in the heavenly sanctuary that answers to the Tabernacle altar of incense. We read in Revelation 5:8, 'Now when He had taken the scroll, the four living creatures and the twenty-four elders fell down before the Lamb, each having a harp, and golden bowls full of incense, which are the prayers of the saints'. Again in Revelation 8:3,4, 'Then another angel, having a golden censer, came and stood at the altar. He was given much incense, that he should offer it with the prayers of all the saints upon the golden altar which was before the throne. And the smoke of the incense, with the prayers of the saints, ascended before God from the angel's hand'.

Heaven has golden bowls full of incense; the prayers of the saints in their fragrance to God. Heaven has golden bowls full of incense; the prayers of the saints in their fragrance to God. Heaven has also a golden censer with much incense, and the prayers from the bowls are added to it and together in their fragrance they reach God.

So all the prayers of all the saints will reach the Father in due course, though some may lie in the golden bowls longer than others, as in the case of Zacharias and Elisabeth.

> Unanswered yet? the pray'r your lips have pleaded
>
> In agony of heart these many years?
>
> Does faith begin to fail? Is hope departing?
>
> And think you all in vain those falling tears?
>
> Say not the Father hath not heard your prayer,
>
> You shall have your desire, sometime, somewhere.
>
> (R. Browning, RS 776)

Faith grasps the fact that, foreshadowed in the altar of incense made of acacia wood but overlaid with pure gold, having the crown and the horns, was the glorious New Testament truth of the Lord Jesus Christ, high and lifted up in resurrection power and glory; interceding in a priestly ministry before the throne of God; the fragrance of His Person giving acceptance to all our prayers. First He would come in the likeness of men, in sinless humanity In the days of His flesh He would share in the experiences of the human family. He would know what was involved in suffering in doing the will of God in a hostile world. He would live in the family circle of a humble, hard-working household and would Himself be a carpenter by trade. He would feel the sorrow of bereavement in His own home, and be misunderstood by His own brothers. He would come through everything that would prepare Him for priestly service; One who would be able to bear gently with the ignorant and erring; One who had suffered being tempted, and thus be able to give help to those who are being tempted; One who had passed our way.

After His victory at Calvary, the Lord Jesus returned on high to the Father's side, crowned as a Priest on the throne, with all power and universal authority, named of God a High Priest after the order of Melchizedek. There before the throne He is the one Mediator between God and men, Himself Man, Christ Jesus (1 Tim.2:5). There He is the Advocate on behalf of all God's children, Jesus Christ the righteous (1 John 2:1). There He is a merciful and faithful High Priest in things pertaining to God, to make propitiation for the sins of His people (Heb.2:17).

All prayer to God is presented through Him. In John 16:23-26 the Lord Jesus spoke of it as asking in His name. That '... name is ointment poured forth' (Song of Songs 1:3). There is no provision in the services of the New Testament churches of God for the burning of incense, a matter in which certain ecclesiastical movements today greatly err. That belonged to the days of the shadows when fire from the bronze altar set free the fragrance from the incense. Even then it was, to God, the fragrance of the coming One which filled the Holy Place. Today it is the reality of His death on the Cross that gives fragrance and acceptance to all collective prayer in God's house.

When we feel hot, burning appreciation of what it cost the Son of God to bring us near, then prayer becomes real, matters for prayer become manifold, and to be present at the assembly prayers is an earnest conviction. Just as the incense was associated with prayer in Old Testament times, so the present position is beautifully pictured in Revelation 8:3, where the prayers of the saints are seen reaching the Father in the acceptance of the fragrance of His beloved Son.

The lampstand shone its light on the priest as he offered the incense at the golden altar in the Tabernacle. Similarly, in God's spiritual house today, the light shines clearly on this very lovely truth of collective prayer by the people of God in the Name of the Lord Jesus Christ.

THE PARABLE OF THE TABERNACLE

The early disciples continued steadfastly in the prayers. This new dispensational feature was an exercise greatly enjoyed and engaged in by them. They experienced the unique power that came from it (see Acts 4:23-31; Acts 12:5; Rom.15:30; 2 Cor.1:11; Phil.1:19 and other portions). The churches were strengthened by such messages as,

'... continuing steadfastly in prayer' (Rom.12:12);

'praying always ... in the Spirit' (Eph.6:18);

'pray without ceasing' (1 Thess.5:17).

They were encouraged by the Spirit's call, 'Let us therefore come boldly to the throne of grace, that we may obtain mercy and find grace to help in time of need' (Heb.4:16). Not only was continual prayer vital for them, but it was also an entitlement to which God looked forward continually, just as He had stipulated for the perpetual incense in Tabernacle days. We thank God for those who continue steadfastly in the weekly prayers of the churches today. They see the need for communion with God in their own fellowship of supplications, prayers, intercessions, thanksgivings for all men and so forth. They realize also that in the collective testimony of the churches mutual prayer is the lifeline, and they come week by week with some special exercise of faith to lay, as it were, on the golden censer in the Father's presence. May the Lord enable us all to give high priority in our lives to continual fellowship in prayer, with, as we assemble, that personal appreciation in our hearts of which sometimes we sing:

> Before the throne of God above
>
> I have a strong, a perfect plea -
>
> A great High Priest, whose name is Love,
>
> Who ever lives and pleads for me.

My name is graven on His hands;

My name is written on His heart;

I know that while in heaven He stands,

No tongue can bid me hence depart.

(C.L. Bancroft, PHSS 266)

Dr. A.B. Simpson gives a remarkable example of the power of collective prayer[9]: 'The writer saw a very striking illustration of this in the city of Rangoon. Here the largest and finest bell in the East is the particular pride of the great Buddhist Temple, Shwee-da-gone. This bell had been sunk in the river during one of the Anglo-Burman wars, and unavailing efforts had been made by various engineers to raise it. At last a clever native priest asked permission to make the attempt on the condition that the bell be given to his temple. He then had his assistants gather an immense number of bamboo rods. These hollow, light rods can scarcely be kept from floating on water. These bamboo rods were taken down one by one by divers, and fastened to the bell at the bottom of the river. After many thousands of them had been securely fastened, it was noticed that the bell began to move: and when the last bamboo rod had been added, the buoyancy of the accumulated rods was so great, that they actually lifted the enormous mass of bronze from the soot and mire of the river bottom, and bore it to the surface of the stream.

So faith can lift the heaviest burdens and the highest mountains. Every whisper of believing prayer is like one of the little bamboo rods. For a time they seem to be in vain, but there comes a last breath of believing supplication, and lo, the walls of Jericho fall, the mountain becomes a plain, the host of Amalek is defeated. It is the hand upon the throne.

Will you help to maintain this collective prayer exercise to 'keep the incense burning there'?

CHAPTER 22: THE ARK AND THE MERCY SEAT

Exodus 25:10-22; 37:1-9

We come now to the climax of all Tabernacle study. In the Most Holy Place was the ark of the Testimony known later as the ark of the covenant, with the golden mercy seat and the two cherubim of one piece with it. There was nothing else there, certainly no image of God. The experience of Moses at Horeb was to be the experience of the high priest on the annual Day of Atonement:

'You ... saw no form' (Deut.4:12). Yet God was there, for God is Spirit, and here was the place of His throne (Ezek.43:7). Normally no foot of man was ever to enter, save only the high priest one day in the year. Here God dwelt alone with Christ in the shadows of the richest types. The covering cherubim looked down, figuratively, on the atoning blood on the mercy seat and were at rest.

The glory of God appears to have filled the sacred place. It is frequently referred to as the Shekinah glory, an expression not found in Scripture. The word shekinah is the transliteration of a Hebrew word meaning 'to dwell'. And when '... the glory of the LORD filled the tabernacle' then a cloud to correspond had '... covered the tabernacle of meeting' (Ex.40:34). It was a sign that God was now dwelling among His people and Israel saw outside the token of the glory within. For a similar expression of the glory-cloud and the inner glory in Israel's later history see Ezekiel 43:1-5.

The ark was first known as the ark of the Testimony, for the two tablets of the unbroken law placed inside it were known as the Testimony (Ex.25:16). They testified, or witnessed, to what God required of Israel in the covenant of Sinai. But the name ceased in Scripture when they reached the waters of Jordan and were about to enter the land, for then the glories of Canaan were no longer a matter of witness and faith but of glorious realization (Josh.4:16-18).

The name 'ark of the covenant' first occurs in the remarkable context of Numbers 10:33 and is thereafter the usual name for the sacred chest. Again the connection is with the Ten Commandments of the covenant. When Moses saw the sin of Israel it says that he threw down '... the two tablets of the Testimony' and they lay broken somewhere at the foot of Sinai (Ex.32:15-19).

Later, on God's instructions, he wrote upon fresh tablets '... the words of the covenant, the Ten Commandments' (Ex.34:28). The ark measured two and a half cubits in length, and one and a half cubits in breadth and height. The ark was the first requirement of God in all the details of the Tabernacle construction. It was God reaching out from within, a principle He followed also in other circumstances in Leviticus 1:1-6:7. The ark measured two and a half cubits in length, and one and a half cubits in breadth and height. It was made of acacia wood and specifically stated to be overlaid with pure gold both outside and inside. It had a moulding of gold, round about the top, securing the mercy seat in place. It had four rings of gold, one on each 'foot' of the ark, placed on the outside so that the staves of acacia wood overlaid with gold could be placed through them for carrying by the Kohathites when the camp was on the march.

Normally the staves were never to be moved from their place. Ideally once erected, the ark was never to be handled again. When the camp began to march, Aaron and his sons took down the veil and covered the ark with it. Then they laid badger skins over it and spread above a cloth entirely of blue (Num.4:5,6). Only during this operation were the staves to be temporarily taken out for covering, then replaced for carrying. Nothing else in the procession was covered outwardly in blue so the ark was absolutely distinctive in the march, foreshadowing Christ as 'Lord of all' (Acts 10:36).

The two tablets of the law were first placed within the ark, and there were later added what the writer to the Hebrews knew to be '... the golden pot that had the manna' (Heb.9:4) (this dates from Ex.16:34) and '... Aaron's rod that budded' (op. cit.)

The mercy seat, a slab of pure gold, two cubits and a half long and one cubit and a half broad, was placed above the ark, thus fitting exactly within the crown round the ark. (dating from Num.17:10). But, by the time the ark reached its final resting place in Solomon's Temple, it was found to contain only the two tables of the law. Both the manna and the rod had strong associations with murmuring among the people and it may be all trace of this was to be left behind in the temple era.

The mercy seat was sprinkled with blood on the Day of Atonement and there God said He would meet with Moses and commune with him on all matters in which he was to instruct the people.

The mercy seat, a slab of pure gold, two cubits and a half long and one cubit and a half broad, was placed above the ark, thus fitting exactly within the crown round the ark. No depth is given. Of one piece with the mercy seat were two cherubim of hammered gold, one at each end. They were formed facing each other, with their wings spread out on high, both their faces and their wings being directed towards the mercy seat and covering it. The mercy seat was sprinkled with blood on the Day of Atonement and there God said He would meet with Moses and commune with him on all matters in which he was to instruct the people.

It is intensely solemn to consider God thus dwelling among a sinful people, enthroned between the cherubim in the Most Holy Place. Inside the ark were the ten words of the covenant of Sinai, broken every day in the camp of Israel outside. There in the chest they lay unbroken, strong in their condemnation of the sin of the people. But they were covered by the golden mercy seat. The Hebrew word simply means a lid or cover, but the thought behind the cover is a covering for sin; an appeasement, an atonement. It was Luther, in his German translation of the Scriptures, who first introduced the pleasant thought of a mercy seat. Precious covering lid, all of gold but stained with blood, telling of a forgiveness that had no depths. The two cherubim seemed as though they were looking down on the sprinkled blood.

They were symbolic of creatures of the highest intelligence in the angelic order. Ezekiel saw one of their number cover the throne of God (Ezek.28:14), when Satan was among them. They appeared again at Eden at the Fall, guarding the holiness and righteousness of God. Now they are in the camp of Israel, looking down, figuratively speaking, on the requirements of God's holiness in the two tables in the ark. But there is a slab of gold between, a mercy seat sprinkled with blood. The holiness of God found an interim answer in the sprinkled blood. God was meantime passing over sin in His forbearance. The blood of animals insensible to the will of God could never take away sin. But One was coming whose delight would be to do the Father's will. That wonderful life would give such value to His blood (Lev.17:11) that by means of it complete and final remission of sins forever would become possible.

It is written in Exodus 37:1 that '... Bezalel made the ark'. The making of only one other article is attributed to this Spirit-filled craftsman. Gesenius in his Hebrew Lexicon gives the meaning of his name as 'In the shadow, i.e., the protection, of God'. What profound foreshadowings lie here. Great was the mystery of godliness when the Word was manifest in the flesh. The mighty Gabriel told the Galilean virgin that she would bear a Son '... called the Son of the Highest' (Luke 1:32) and that it would be in this way, 'The Holy Spirit will come upon you, and the

THE PARABLE OF THE TABERNACLE 119

power of the Highest will overshadow you' (Luke 1:35). So, in the shadows, Bezalel made the ark.

The ark had 'feet', the derivative thought being steps in walking. The ark was in measurement two cubits and a half by a cubit and a half. Luke describes the position so beautifully;

'... the Babe' (Luke 2:16);

'... the Child' (Luke 2:27);

'... the Boy' (Luke 2:43);

'... Jesus increased' (Luke 2:52);

'... the Man' (Luke 23:6).

It was the eternal Son in the measurements of time. His goings forth were from of old, from everlasting; but now He was in '... the days of His flesh' (Heb.5:7), bounded by time and years. The Man of the acacia wood was overlaid within and without with gold. Whether searched by the eye of God or man, every thought and action was in absolute agreement with His divine nature. After the thirty home years in Nazareth, God said at His baptism, 'This is My beloved Son, in whom I am well pleased' (Matt.3:17). The astonished Israelites said, 'He has done all things well' (Mark 7:37). The hard Roman centurion said, '... Truly this was the Son of God!' (Matt.27:54).

The law of the Ten Commandments was kept unbroken in two places only; one was in the type, the ark; the other was in the true, the Person of the Lord Jesus Christ. He inspired David to describe His own feelings in Psalm 40:8, 'I delight to do Your will, O my God, and Your law is within my heart'. After the years of His earthly service, in which He was bombarded by Satan, He was rejected by those on whom He had bestowed healing and affection, betrayed by one of His closest followers and deserted by the rest. Contemptuously despised and put to brutal shame by His Roman captors, He came at last to Calvary in all the strength of the unbroken law. Loving His God with all His heart, soul, strength and mind, and His neighbour as Himself, He offered Himself willingly to make the atonement, and thus establish the basis for reconciliation between God and the human family. There the One whom God set forth from all eternity to be a propitiation was set forth for all to see (Rom.3: 25). It was as though the great anti-type of the mercy seat, hidden behind the veil, was brought forth from the divine presence that men might see Him make the atonement.

Then, in the glory of the resurrection, He took His Manhood back with Him to the throne of God. That throne is known as a throne of grace today. The grace of the Lord Jesus Christ has given it this character. In the glory of the eternal state it will be known as the throne of God and of the Lamb. It is the death of the Lamb that will give eternal stability to it. It will be, as it were, a blood-sprinkled throne, as foreshadowed in the Most Holy Place in the Tabernacle. Now on heaven's throne, He is Himself the great Mercy Seat, the great basis for the covering and remission of sin of all those who flee to Him for refuge. It is on the ground of a mercy that is all of God, absolutely fathomless in the abundance of its pardon and endless in its effect even though there were ends to the mercy seat in the Most Holy Place. It is made available, blood stained, to the repentant sinner. For He is Himself the '... propitiation [i.e., the mercy seat] by His blood, through faith' (Rom.3:25).

Little wonder the principalities and the powers in the heavenly places look on and wonder at the marvellous outworking of the manifold wisdom of God (Eph.3:10); peering into it as the shadowy cherubim in the Most Holy Place seemed to peer at the blood-stained slab. There, in the presence of God, the Man who once walked here in the power of an unbroken law, can give to His people a divine enabling to fulfil the ordinances of that law by walking in the power of the Spirit. He can be to

THE PARABLE OF THE TABERNACLE 121

them the hidden manna, communion-food corresponding to the golden pot with its contents within the ark. He can be to them a Priest for their help, no matter what their age group or spiritual progress, corresponding to the priestly rod inside the ark that had budded, produced blossoms and yielded ripe almonds.

For some 500 years the old Tabernacle, the great original visual aid of the house of God on the sandy desert floor, continued its chequered and mainly sorrowful way with the nation of Israel. After nearly 400 years God had to desert it in the days of Eli (Ps.78:60,61) when the nation in its wickedness desecrated the sanctuary by entering the Most Holy Place and taking out to battle the sacred '... ark of the covenant of the LORD of hosts, who dwells between the cherubim' (1 Sam.4:4).

He never allowed His ark back into the Tabernacle. It went first to the house of Abinadab in the hill, where it remained until David removed it to the special tent he had erected for it (2 Sam.6:17). The ark with its ministry under Asaph was in the tent in Jerusalem; the Tabernacle with its altar of burnt offering and attendant services in the high place at Gibeon (see 1 Chr.16:37-43). Then in due course the ark was taken from the tent of David to the Temple of Solomon. This dark era in Israel's national history, when it must have been impossible to carry out the detailed ritual of the vital Day of Atonement, covered the period 1 Samuel 4 to 1 Kings 8, probably in excess of 100 years.

At last David's dream was realized and Solomon's Temple was completed. David had envisaged it as '... a house of rest for the ark of the covenant of the LORD', '... a house for the sanctuary', '... the place of the mercy seat' (1 Chr.28:2,10,11). So '... they brought up the ark of the LORD, the tabernacle of meeting, and all the holy furnishings that were in the tabernacle' (1 Kin.8:4).

It would seem as though they selected the ark and probably removed the old dismantled Tabernacle and its accessories to one of the treasuries of the temple. But they brought the ark into its place in the inner sanctuary of the new temple, in the choice setting of 2 Chronicles 5 and to the accompaniment of the delightful words of 2 Chronicles 6:41. 'Now therefore, arise, O LORD God, to Your resting place, You and the ark of Your strength'.

Among David's last words were these, '... also to the Levites, "They shall no longer carry the tabernacle, or any of the articles for its service"' (1 Chr.23:26). So the RV marginal reading of 1 Kings 8:8 makes pleasant reading, in connection with the ark, 'And they drew out the staves'. Travelling days were over.

In keeping with the type, Christ is still being borne on the shoulders of dedicated disciples for others around to see. God's first description of the future life of service of Saul of Tarsus was, '... he is a chosen vessel of Mine to bear My name before Gentiles, kings, and the children of Israel' (Acts 9:15).

But no priest bore the ark of the testimony alone. The staves ensured fellowship in service. Beloved Paul bore his Master's Name all the remaining years of his life in a fellowship of service with others, in the fellowship of the churches of God, in '... the fellowship of His Son, Jesus Christ our Lord' (1 Cor.1:9). Many today are being led by the Spirit in an earnest endeavour to follow his '... doctrine, manner of life, purpose, faith, longsuffering, love, perseverance, persecutions, afflictions' (2 Tim.3:10,11).

We write to encourage one another. The testimony is still being '... testified in due time' (1 Tim.2:6). But days of testimony-bearing may soon be over, and the staves will be drawn out. The word comes again to us from Ezekiel 43:10, 'Son of man, describe the temple to the house of Israel ... and let them measure the pattern'.

The house of God is a place of unique position in which disciples of the Lord Jesus Christ may find themselves today. We have briefly touched on salient features of the pattern; briefly 'shown' it. We would warmly encourage beloved fellow-believers to whom some of the teachings of the house of God may be unfamiliar to weigh up the matter carefully, prayerfully before the Lord. Measure the pattern.

The house of God is also a place calling for a right spiritual condition, for Jacob's vision has at last come in reality, and God's spiritual house is the very gate of heaven; a holy priesthood assembling on the earth, but drawing near to worship in the sanctuary in heaven. To all readers who enjoy, or who may aspire to a place in God's house, we would re-emphasize the imperative need for the eyes of the Lord and of all our contacts, to see in us continually the bright shining gold of the divine nature in a day of ever-increasing spiritual darkness.

---

[1] Fairbairn, P. 1854 Typology of Scripture, Vol. 2 (2nd ed.). Smith and English, Philadelphia, p.234.

[2] Pusey, E.B. 1860-1871. The Minor Prophets with a Commentary Explanatory and Practical and Introductions to the several Books. Parts i, iv, Hosea to Nahum. Oxford: Parker & Co.

[3] Josephus, F. The complete works of Flavius Josephus translated by Whiston W., 1856. T. Nelson and Sons, London; Edinburgh; and New York 856 pp. See Antiquities of the Jews, Book 3, chapter 6 sections 4 p.88 and 8, p.89.

[4] Strong, J. 1890. Exhaustive Concordance of the Bible.

[5] Luxmoore, C. M. L. 1899. The coupling together of assemblies, Needed Truth pp. 242-252.

[6] Kennedy, A.R.S. in Hastings, J. (ed.) 1898-1902, A Dictionary of the Bible. 4 vols and supplementary vol. 1904; 1 vol. edition 1909. Edinburgh, T.&T. Clark; New York, Charles Scribner's Sons.

[7] Wuest, K.S. 1956-1959. Wuest's Expanded translation of the Greek New Testament Re-published 1961 (and reprinted 1994) as The New Testament: An Expanded Translation. Eerdmans, Grand Rapids.

[8] Douglas, J.D. 1962 (Organizing Editor), New Bible Dictionary (Kept 1972). London: Inter-varsity Press, 1775 pp. esp. p. 1323.

[9] i) Simpson, A.B. The Alliance Weekly, October 1912, pp. 35-36.

Did you love *The Parable of the Tabernacle*? Then you should read *An Introduction to the Book of Hebrews* by Hayes Press!

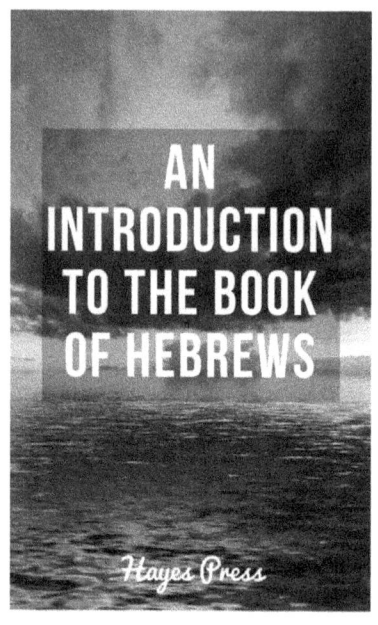

This book provides a concise introduction to the New Testament book of Hebrews, perhaps one of the least understood books in the Bible, yet it provides a unique and valuable insight into the meaning of Old Testament tabernacle worship for Christians today!CHAPTER ONE: THE LORD'S DEITY AND HUMANITY (PART 1)CHAPTER TWO: THE LORD'S DEITY AND HUMANITY (PART 2)CHAPTER THREE: GOD'S HOUSE AND GOD'S RESTCHAPTER FOUR: HIGH PRIEST AFTER THE ORDER OF MELCHIZEDEKCHAPTER FIVE: THE TYPICAL TEACHING OF THE AARONIC PRIESTHOODCHAPTER SIX: FALLING AWAYCHAPTER SEVEN: THE WAY OF THE HOLIESCHAPTER EIGHT: FAITH'S VISION OF THE UNSEENCHAPTER NINE: RUN WITH PATIENCECHAPTER TEN:

MOUNT ZION AND THE HEAVENLY JERUSALEMCHAPTER ELEVEN: OUTSIDE THE CAMPCHAPTER TWELVE: A CONCLUDING REVIEW

About the Publisher

Hayes Press (www.hayespress.org) is a registered charity in the United Kingdom, whose primary mission is to disseminate the Word of God, mainly through literature. It is one of the largest distributors of gospel tracts and leaflets in the United Kingdom, with over 100 titles and hundreds of thousands despatched annually. In addition to paperbacks and eBooks, Hayes Press also publishes Plus Eagles Wings, a fun and educational Bible magazine for children, and Golden Bells, a popular daily Bible reading calendar in wall or desk formats. Also available are over 100 Bibles in many different versions, shapes and sizes, Bible text posters and much more!

www.ingramcontent.com/pod-product-compliance
Lightning Source LLC
Chambersburg PA
CBHW031402040426
42444CB00005B/384